A PORTRAIT OF SHERIDAN

Richard Brinsley Sheridan, studio of Joshua Reynolds *c.* 1789.

A · PORTRAIT · OF
SHERIDAN

STANLEY AYLING

CONSTABLE · LONDON

First published in Great Britain 1985
by Constable and Company Limited
10 Orange Street London WC2H 7EG
Copyright © 1985 by Stanley Ayling
ISBN 0 09 465380 1
Set in Monophoto Ehrhardt 11pt by
Servis Filmsetting Ltd, Manchester
Printed in Great Britain by
St Edmundsbury Press
Bury St Edmunds, Suffolk

British Library CIP data
Ayling, Stanley
A portrait of Sheridan
1. Sheridan, Richard Brinsley–Biography
2. Dramatists, English–19th century–
Biography
I. Title
822'.6   PR3683

ISBN 0 09 465380 1

For Kirsty, Zoë, and Lucy

Contents

Illustrations

Foreword

SHERIDAN, the leading British dramatist of the eighteenth century, became so by force of genius perhaps, but by quirks of circumstance certainly. At twenty-three he was more or less penniless and married to a beautiful and distinguished singer possessed of a small fortune. Honour forbade that he should live off her income – forbade even that he should allow her to continue to earn by singing. He looked therefore in various directions and eventually settled upon the theatre, with which, though it did not much attract him, he had some acquaintance. His father was an actor and had been a theatre manager. Sheridan then wrote a comic opera and three plays – only three of much consequence – and by them became as celebrated as his wife, and made a little money. This he gambled (together with much more that he borrowed) by investing it in the theatre business, thereby gaining a source of bread and butter but also involvement in financial tangles from which he was never to escape.

But no man was ever *less* stage-struck than Sheridan. He once claimed that he had never in his whole life managed to sit through one play from beginning to end. Just how strong were his feelings, or prejudices, against the stage even after his first success with *The Rivals*, emerges from a very long and passionately argued letter he wrote to the man who had recently become his father-in-law, Thomas Linley of Bath, one of the leading musicians and concert-promoters of his day. Sheridan begged Linley not to allow his second daughter Mary (Polly) to become an actress under Garrick's management.

He could see nothing wrong in Linley's employing his daughters on the concert platform. Indeed Maria, the third daughter, was already launched with her father as a singer, and Sheridan recognized that her reputation was 'spreading amazingly'. But *acting* for a girl from a respectable family – a thousand times no. 'No gentleman of character and fortune ever yet', he declared, 'took a wife from behind the scenes of a theatre.' A singer 'under the wings of her parent' was one thing; an actress, 'the unblushing object of a licentious gaping croud', was quite another, 'the creature of a mercenary manager, the servant of the town, and a licens'd mark for libertinism'.

> What is the *modesty* of any woman whose trade it is eternally to represent all the different modifications of love before a mix'd assembly of rakes, whores, lords and blackguards in succession! – to play the coquet, the wanton, to retail loose innuendos in comedy, or glow with warm descriptions in tragedy; and in both to be haul'd about, squeez'd and kiss'd by beastly pimping actors! – what is to be the fate of a girl of seventeen in such a situation? – what of a girl of Polly's particular attractions?

In short, alleged Sheridan, the stage was 'the greatest nursery of vice and misery on the face of the earth'.

Gentlemen and players

RICHARD BRINSLEY SHERIDAN was born at 12 Dorset Street, a spacious and fairly new house in the then-fashionable northern district of Dublin. The year was 1751, but the precise date of his birth has never been established. The parish register witnesses that he was baptized in November of that year, curiously as *Thomas* Brinsley. Either the clergyman erred, which is improbable, or Sheridan's parents decided later to call him, not after his father and grandfather, both Thomases, but after one or the other of his uncles Richard. The 'Brinsley' was a family name of the Earl of Lanesborough who stood godfather. Richard was the third, and eventually the second surviving, son of Frances Sheridan (1724–1766), soon to be a modestly successful novelist and playwright, and of Thomas Sheridan (1719–1788) actor-manager, grammarian, lecturer in rhetoric or 'oratory', educational theorist, theatrical and literary jack-of-all-trades. Four of their six children survived infancy: Charles, Richard, Alicia (Lissy), and Anne Elizabeth (Betsy, by five years the youngest).

Frances Sheridan's forebears came from England; she was the daughter of a prebendary and archdeacon of the Church of Ireland (that is, of course, the Church of England in Ireland) and granddaughter of an English baronet, Sir Oliver Chamberlaine. Sheridan's father, Thomas, and Sheridan himself in after years laid equal but rather more speculative claim to gentle extraction.

[15]

Thomas Sheridan, moving professionally on the fringes of the genteel and aristocratic world, always resented the imputation that he was just 'a player', and Richard Brinsley Sheridan, in his schooldays at Harrow among the sons of the rich, was soon to find that it was unfortunate to be known to be a 'poor player's son'. Thomas Sheridan, as his grand-daughter Alicia Lefanu was to insist (in her *Memoirs of Mrs Frances Sheridan* of 1824), was 'a gentleman both by birth and education'. This was in rebuttal of a recently published slur that the Sheridans were a family 'possessing neither pedigree nor property'. Thomas's father Thomas (1687–1738), whatever his pedigree, had certainly been a scholar of distinction. Doctor of divinity, schoolmaster, author, and eccentric, he had been until he quarrelled the friend of Swift (who, indeed, called him 'the best instructor of youth in the three kingdoms, and perhaps in Europe'); though whether his residence at Quilca in County Cavan boasted 'a considerable property' or was, rather, the aggrandisement of a cottage permitted, and permits, a difference of opinion. It was this grandfather of Sheridan's who once committed the delightful impropriety of preaching, on the anniversary of the accession of the House of Hanover, upon the text 'Sufficient unto the day is the evil thereof', an act, whether of snook-cocking or simple carelessness, which cost him his living and chaplaincy to the Lord Lieutenant.

Sheridan always remained sensitive, in that age obsessed by rank, to suggestions that the gentlemanly status of his origins was suspect. He might joke perhaps about his ancestors the O'Sheridans of County Cavan, but the joke was more than half serious, and he certainly preferred to give his lineage the benefit of any doubt whether it did or did not trace descent from the sixteenth-century Donald O'Sheridan, 'of Cloughloughter Castle and Balliconnel Castle in County Cavan'.*

Sheridan's father had been sent to Westminster School at fourteen, but was withdrawn early, from *his* father's inability to

---

* Sheridan's elder son once observed that his father had every right to be known as O'Sheridan, since he *owed* everybody.

provide the necessary fees. By the age of seventeen he was at Trinity College, Dublin, fired with the two passions which were to dominate his intellectual and professional career: one, the supreme importance of good English, written and spoken (a conviction which from the earliest years his father and his godfather Dean Swift had laboured to instil), and the other, the world of the theatre. At twenty-three, heralded on the playbills as a 'young gentleman', he achieved instant success playing Richard III at Dublin's Theatre Royal, Smock Alley; was soon playing Hamlet and other leading roles at Covent Garden; and by his middle twenties was back in charge at Smock Alley, ambitious to present 'good and chaste' plays.

'In charge' somewhat overstates his situation. Smock Alley proved too often to be in the hands of either its noisy gallery (admission twopence) or its disorderly young bloods downstairs. These, Dublin's young men of fashion, not content with forming a turbulent audience, were inclined to exercise their gentleman's privilege of making free of the backstage and green-room, and of pestering the actresses. Half the place was a bear-garden, declared Thomas Sheridan, and the other half a brothel. Against the ill will of some of these fashionable bravos who objected to being dictated to by a mere 'player', he tried to insist at least on having the stage kept clear during performances. But during 1746–7, conditions at Smock Alley, as the then Trinity undergraduate Edmund Burke reported, became dangerously explosive. In 'the grand theatrical squabble between Mr Kelly gentleman and Sheridan the player' which had 'divided the town into two parties as violent as whig and tory' (so Burke wrote to a friend) the Trinity men had 'engaged themselves on Sheridan's side'. (Unfortunately this support was not to last.) One night in February 1746

Mr Kelly comes in flush'd with liquor and going into the green room where the players dress began to entertain the actresses with the most nauseous bawdry and ill language cal[led] them bitches and whores put his hand under their

[17]

petticoats and would have forced some of them (if his ability answer'd his inclination).

Enraged at being ordered out of the house by Sheridan, Kelly 'as soon as Sheridan came on the stage pelted him with oranges . . . and call'd him a thousand ill names'. Afterwards, going to the manager's room, he was given a flogging by Sheridan. To revenge this indignity, the following night Kelly brought along some dozens of his supporters who took it 'extremely ill that a gentleman should be struck by a player', broke open the doors, stopped the show, and (says Burke) would probably have killed Sheridan if he had not escaped. Various court proceedings ensued, and Kelly was fined and briefly imprisoned.

One odd but happy consequence for Thomas Sheridan of this conflict with the Kelly faction turned out to be marriage. He was shown some very presentable verses and an article in praise of his conduct written by a young lady who proved on enquiry to be the daughter of the late Archdeacon Chamberlaine. In 1747 he married her, and by 1751, when Richard Brinsley made his entrance, she had borne him three sons. During these years of the late 1740s and early '50s Thomas Sheridan continued his uphill struggle to make the Theatre Royal, Smock Alley 'a school for manners and virtue', and in this he was for some time notably successful. Georgian Dublin, now in the heyday of the Protestant ascendancy, was a proud and lively place, arguably 'the fifth capital in Europe' and certainly the second city of the British Isles. Under the patronage of the Lord Lieutenant and the management now of Thomas Sheridan, its playhouse provided theatrical entertainment hardly, if at all, inferior to that of Drury Lane and Covent Garden, and many of the finest players of the day, Garrick, Foote, Thomas Sheridan himself, Mrs Bellamy, and Dublin's own Peg Woffington among them, headed the Smock Alley playbills. Surveying his personal achievement later, at a time when a salvo of self-justification was excusable, Thomas Sheridan claimed moreover that there was not 'a more polite or decent assembly in Europe' than was generally to be found in his playhouse. On a rising tide of professional and social acceptance he went on to found a Dublin Beefsteak Club, emulating the Covent Garden manager John Rich with his Sublime Society of Steaks. Each week in his Dorset Street dining-room Thomas Sheridan would entertain at his own expense some thirty or forty of Dublin's men of letters, wits, artists, and politicians, including sometimes the Duke of Dorset himself, Lord Lieutenant, and often at head of table, as President and only woman member, the captivating Mrs Woffington.

Unluckily Thomas Sheridan's apparently so desirable and so well advertised association with King George's viceroy and the ruling political party was his undoing. If he was such a friend of the Dublin Castle establishment, the patriotic party were out to punish him for it; and in March 1754 they wrecked his auditorium, curtains, stage, and backstage, from which last he fled – first, to take immediate refuge at his home in Dorset Street, and then to abandon his Smock Alley management in disgust. He let the theatre, refused the Lord Lieutenant's offer of a handsome pension with reparation for damages suffered, moved to Bedford Street in London, and for a time acted leading parts at neighbouring Covent Garden. There, however, he experienced the insuperable handicap of being compared unfavourably with Garrick at Drury Lane, and a certain jealousy of Garrick's enormous success never afterwards left him. Mrs Sheridan, whose latest child, her fourth, had just died in infancy, followed her husband to London, but she did not take the two-year-old Richard with her. He, with his older brother Charles, was left behind in Dublin in the care of relations and a nurse.

But to Dublin Thomas Sheridan returned in two years' time, in another attempt to revive the fortunes of Smock Alley and his own reputation as actor and manager; and this time too as president and prime mover in a 'Hibernian Society' which proposed to run educational lectures and generally encourage Dublin culture to raise its sights. In these various projects he ran up considerable debts which were to prove a serious future embarrassment. And luck was not with him at Smock Alley, particularly as a rival theatre opened in Crow Street under Spranger Barry. Thomas Sheridan was defeated again.

Now therefore he sought a substitute livelihood with that other obsessive interest of his, the role of correct speech and writing in the education of the nobility and gentry. This proved to be the beginning of half a lifetime given over to pamphlets, dissertations, discourses, 'humble appeals' to the public, 'Attic entertainments' of taste and sobriety, a two-volume pronouncing dictionary, two volumes on *The Art of Reading*, and much else of a didactic, pedagogical nature aimed at improvement in elocution, oratory, grammar, pronunciation (in which he sought 'a perpetual standard') – and consequently in manners. The characteristic trend of his argument is well suggested in the title of a work he published soon after retiring from his second defeat at Smock Alley: *British Education, or the Sources of the Disorders in Great Britain*.

The young Burke called him an arrogant man, which he may well have been, and ignorant, which he was not. Dr Johnson sniffed at poor 'Sherryderry' both as literary man and lexicographer, and wrote him off as 'dull, naturally dull' – later however conceding that he excelled in declamation, and that 'were mankind to be divided into the good and the bad, he would stand considerably within the ranks of the good'. He was certainly pedantic, self-justifying, opinionated, and vain, with a temperament and intelligence as stiff and dogged as his famous son's were to be spontaneous and mercurial. It is no wonder that their mutual relationship was to be plagued by constant disharmony, resulting with the father in a good deal of fault-finding and resentment, and with the son in lasting sadness.

Sheridan's first experience of schooling came at a new establishment just opened in Grafton Street, Dublin by Samuel Whyte, the natural son of Mrs Sheridan's uncle. Sheridan attended this 'seminary' with his young sister Lissy during the period when his parents were away in London, between the two Smock Alley ventures. 'I have all a mother's anxiety about them, and long to have them over with me,' wrote Mrs Sheridan; and by the time Dick was eight (by then Mrs Sheridan had had a second daughter, Betsy) the temporary orphans were able to join their parents in London, where the elder boy Charles already was. Sheridan's education, and no doubt that of the other children too, was for the next year or two in the hands exclusively of his parents, and of his father in particular. By 1762 he was ready to be sent as a boarder to Harrow where he was to spend the next six years.

Thomas Sheridan chose Harrow because he had recently made the acquaintance of Dr Sumner, the newly appointed headmaster. While on a summer stay at Windsor he had met Sumner, then in his last months as an Eton assistant, and had taken to him. Only Dick, not Charles, was to have the privilege, and undergo as it proved the ordeals, of a Harrow education, and some words of Frances Sheridan at this time tell us why. 'Charles's domestic and sedentary turn', she wrote, 'is best suited to a home education,' but as for Dick, since 'he may probably fall into a bustling life, we have a mind to accustom him to shift for himself'. Sedentary Charles, bustling Dick. Charles: more malleable? an apter subject to profit from his father's educational prospectus? Dick: already with greater signs of spirit and independence? The two boys, the two men, would always be oil and water, chalk and cheese; and relations between them would turn out no warmer than those between Sheridan and his father.

Life at Harrow was soon to put Sheridan's 'bustle' and self-reliance through some daunting tests. As he told the diarist Thomas Creevey half a century later, he became for a time a very 'low-spirited' small boy. He was obliged to 'shift for himself' indeed. For one thing, as he recounted to Creevey, he was often not able to go home in the holidays. This was true even during his first two years; it became inevitable when his parents decided in 1764 to go to live in France, an apparently surprising move, since the previous year or two had been professionally good for both of them. Mr Sheridan had been granted a pension from the Crown in recognition of his *Dictionary*. Mrs Sheridan's novel *Sidney Biddulph* was excellently received, and her comedy *The Dis-*

covery, with her husband in the cast, made a success at Drury Lane. But the removal to France is explicable partly on grounds of economy – living would be cheaper there – and partly because Thomas Sheridan was being put under dangerous pressure by his Dublin creditors. So the family, all but Dick, settled at Blois in central France, while he was put under the care of his uncle Richard Chamberlaine, a London surgeon.

Thus for a considerable time there *was* no home for Sheridan to go to in the holidays, which were spent either remaining at Harrow or staying with friends of the family. Term-time brought its own tribulations. With his school fees paid very irregularly and his clothes liable to be outgrown or shabby, Sheridan soon became known as not only a player's son – a minus mark in itself – but a *poor* player's son and so an easy victim of unpleasantnesses which he never forgot. 'Slighted by the masters and tormented by the boys,' was the version of these misfortunes offered some half-century later by Charles Fox's nephew, Lord Holland, who also recounted that Sheridan – the by then elderly, bibulous, sometimes lachrymose Sheridan – had 'tears in his eyes' as he told Holland of them. Allowing that Holland's accounts of Sheridan's character and behaviour are always slightly suspect, the picture is probably still not far from the truth. One is reminded of the young Anthony Trollope a lifetime later at the same school, though *his* unhappiness sprang additionally from a misfortune far removed from Sheridan's, the social stigma of being a day boy. Home contact and family care were just what the young Sheridan needed and lacked. There are forlorn-sounding hints of loneliness and neglect in a letter written to his acting guardian, Richard Chamberlaine, when Sheridan was thirteen or fourteen (it is the earliest of his letters to have survived):

Dear Uncle

As it is not more than three weeks to the holy days, I should be greatly obliged to you, if you could get me some new cloaths as soon as possible, for those which I have at present are very bad and as I have no others; I am almost ashamed to wear them on a

Sunday. I fancy I shall spend my holy days again at Harrow . . . Mr Somner asked me the other day if I had heard lately from my brother and says he has not heard from them this long time: if you have had a letter lately I should be obliged to you [sic] would let me know how they are and when they come to England for I long to see them . . .

The request for new clothes, repeated in this letter, is made twice again in his next. His brown ones were 'quite gone'; his light-coloured ones, having 'met with a few accidents' were 'not remarkably clean'; and since he was now in the top form he was 'under a necessity of appearing like the other 5 form boys'. (Perhaps it was not really the top form; Samuel Parr, a master at Harrow during Sheridan's last two years there and later headmaster, told Thomas Moore, Sheridan's first biographer, that he 'never reached the Sixth Form'.)

The necessity to beg new clothes is yet again his main concern when he next writes to Richard Chamberlaine four months later, but this time for a more 'melancholly' reason. This time they must be black. Frances Sheridan had died at Blois at the age of forty-two, and her son, just fifteen now, needed 'a new hat with a crape of black and black stokins and buckles', as well as 'a suit of black'. 'You will excuse the shortness of my letter', he concludes, 'as the subject is disagreeable.'

Most of the estimates of Sheridan's scholastic proficiency at Harrow, written long afterwards when he had already become famous, are of dubious value. Even Dr Parr's, less glowing than most, have to be read as those of a man who became a firm friend in later days. He claims that he descried in the young Sheridan 'vestiges of a superior intellect' and that 'somehow or other' his schoolmates accorded him 'esteem and admiration'. On the other hand he told Thomas Moore that Sheridan was 'inferior to his schoolfellows in the ordinary business of a school', and on one occasion when Parr was deputizing for the headmaster Sumner, he found Sheridan 'very defective in Greek Grammar' as he most evidently was also in English spelling and punctuation – and

[23]

remained all his life. His industry, Parr declared, 'was just sufficient to protect him from disgrace . . . His answers to any common question were prompt and acute.' But Parr would have taught Sheridan only very briefly indeed, and of course all that he says relates only to the end of his time at Harrow. By then, no doubt, he had got over his early 'low spirits' and was, as Parr remembered or thought he remembered, cheerful, vivacious, harmlessly mischievous – altogether more like the popular conception of the mature Sheridan.

It is clear that he was no academic wonder and possessed none of that prodigious juvenile scholarship which so delighted the parents and astonished the admirers of his near-contemporaries and future Parliament-men Charles Fox or William Pitt the younger. He would, however, always claim pride in his knowledge of the Greek and Roman authors and loved to grace his oratory, in the conventional eighteenth-century manner, with allusions to them. When in the Commons once, in his forties, he put Lord Belgrave to rights in the matter of a Demosthenes quotation, the very fact that he so often subsequently insisted on recalling that little victory argues perhaps that on that day he surprised himself as much as his auditors – or perhaps merely that his memory was always excellent, and that Demosthenes, like Virgil and Horace, provided one of the classical subjects that Sheridan 'did' quite thoroughly at school.

At the time of his wife's death Thomas Sheridan, with the help of Irish friends, was in the middle of negotiating the practicalities of returning home. He eventually succeeded in placating his creditors and settling his Dublin affairs at least well enough to make his presence there safe from arrest. Back soon afterwards in London, he took a house in Frith Street, Soho; brought his two daughters back from France (since their mother's death they had been lodging at St Quentin); and eventually – at last – assembled all his children under the one paternal roof. Sheridan was to leave Harrow but not to be sent to university. It is said that Dr Parr thought he should have been. His father however may well have considered the educational programme which he himself was prepared – was anxious – to offer both his sons hardly inferior to that of Oxford or Cambridge, and it would certainly be less expensive. To assist him he engaged a tutor for mathematics and Latin, while he himself was to concentrate on the teaching of English and 'oratory'. His own latest *Plan of Education for the Young Nobility and Gentry of Great Britain*, dedicated to George III, was published that year in Dublin and later in London. A pupil of his at this time was the young Henry Angelo, whose father, the great swordsman, in exchange for his son's instruction provided lessons in riding and fencing for both the Sheridan boys at his Soho academy. The second of these accomplishments in particular would soon prove to be of some importance for Sheridan.

Before leaving school he had started writing; and now, in the main a young-man-about-town, he continued to pursue a literary ambition, developing a fluent and agreeable skill in light verse, mildly amorous or gently satirical; turning out essays on current politics with an eye to the public prints (including an ironical defence of the Prime Minister, Grafton, against 'Junius'); collaborating with a Harrow friend, Nathaniel Halhed, by now at Oxford, in a three-act farce tenuously foreshadowing *The Critic* and never staged; proposing a periodical or 'miscellany', also with Halhed, of which number one was written but never issued. Another joint production however did achieve print, though Sheridan's share in it may well have been confined to putting a polish on the verse. This translation, or free paraphrase, from the Greek appeared as *The Love Epistles of Aristaenetus*, Aristaenetus being an author obscure enough to be invisible, whose own work it seems was no more than a refurbishing of that of others such as Lucian and Plutarch.

The Linleys of Bath

THE *Love Epistles* appeared in 1771. By then the Sheridans had left London to lodge in 'a very neat house, pleasantly situated and very cheap' in Kingsmead Street, Bath. This modest situation was forthwith advertised locally by Thomas Sheridan as an Academy ready to instruct Young Gentlemen in reading, reciting, and grammar. His two sons were to act as assistants, and the younger of them looking back in later years (and very probably at the time also) found the project somewhat laughable. It certainly met no favourable wind.

Within a few weeks of the move, Sheridan, in a long and lively letter to Mrs Angelo, the fencing-master's Irish wife, was telling of 'a Mr Linley here, a music master, who has a daughter that sings like an angel'. An angel: nobody ever seems to have spoken of Elizabeth Linley without stressing this angelic quality – whether from the purity and sweetness of her voice, the spirituality of her expression, the tenderness of her disposition, or the fragile perfection of her person. Miss Linley, moreover, as the contemporary Exeter composer William Jackson bore witness, was a highly intelligent singer: 'her genius and sense gave a consequence to her performance which no fool with the voice of an angel could ever attain.' Was Sheridan then already in love with this gifted beauty of sixteen? Only perhaps in the way that a multitude of others were. It was almost a denial of nature

[26]

not to be in love with Miss Linley, and in the course of her performing travels round England she had already collected a small army of suitors. (She remained for Sheridan, despite everything, an 'angel' to the end: it was the inevitable word that sprang to his self-accusing pen in remorseful anguish during her tragic last days.)

Within two months of his arrival in Bath, Elizabeth Linley was providing a share in Thomas Sheridan's further cultural assault upon the city. This was his programme of Attic Entertainments – 'the reading part by Mr Sheridan' (including Dryden's *Ode to St Cecilia*), 'the singing by Miss Linley' (as it were St Cecilia in person). Elizabeth was the most celebrated, but was still only one of a whole concert, of Linleys active in Bath's musical life at the time. In all, Thomas and Maria Linley (she was a musician too) had twelve children, of whom however only two were to live past the age of forty. All those who survived infancy were brought up to be musicians – singers or instrumentalists, and usually both. Thomas Linley himself, the music master, was among the country's most prominent musical all-rounders, composer, conductor, concert-manager. Elizabeth, his eldest daughter, now a veteran of sixteen, had been before an admiring public from the age of twelve. Her sister Mary (Polly), four years younger, was already following a similar path. And Thomas junior, in age half-way between these two sisters and a concert violinist from the age of seven, was a prodigy to bear comparison with the young Mozart, who as it happened was the same age and even, for a time when they were fourteen and both touring Italy, his 'dear friend'. Thomas Linley senior and Mozart's father Leopold were alike too in the way they both regarded their children's genius as a valuably marketable commodity. ('We are all geniuses here, sir,' little Tom Linley is reported as telling a visitor.) Mozart was to die young enough, but Tom Linley younger still, drowned in a boating accident at the age of twenty-two.

In December 1770 an engagement was announced between Elizabeth Linley and Walter Long, a sixty-year-old Wiltshire squire reputed to be worth a quarter of a million. The match was

The Linley sisters, painted by Thomas Gainsborough. Elizabeth (standing), who married Sheridan, was a famous and gifted singer; Mary (seated) later married the writer and satirist Richard Tickell.

approved by Thomas Linley on Long's promise to indemnify him with £1,000 for the loss of the musical services of the girl who, as well as being his daughter, was his indentured apprentice and a prime source of income. In the polite *comme il faut* of the day, it was not acceptable for a professional actress or singer on marrying into the aristocracy or gentry to continue performing for pay, and Elizabeth therefore discontinued platform appearances immediately. The account of what happened then depends substantially upon whether one follows the line of the *London Magazine*, or *Lloyd's Evening Post*, or the *Bath Chronicle*, or Sheridan's niece Alicia Lefanu, or the more scandalous 'real-life' dramatic version entitled *The Maid of Bath*, written hot on the heels of the events by the actor-manager Samuel Foote and staged at the Haymarket Theatre, London. Foote depicted Walter Long as 'Solomon Flint', a 'fusty, shabby, shuffling . . . old hulks', amorous indeed but deterred from matrimony by cautionary tales from his cronies, and then demanding from his 'Kitty Linnet' a premarital token of love before agreeing to go through with the ceremony. If this was a mischievous exaggeration of the true story, at least it was what Foote, Garrick, the dramatist Cumberland, and half London and Bath *believed* to be the truth, and what made Miss Linley and the Maid of Bath one and the same notoriously wronged heroine. Walter Long, not relishing being the talk of the town, retired hurt, breaking off the engagement. When the Linleys threatened him with an action for damages, he settled £3,000 on Elizabeth with a further gift of jewels worth £1,000.

In judging the motives and understanding the conduct of the principals in this affair – the Linley parents, Walter Long, Elizabeth herself – it must be remembered that in Georgian England the person of a public performer as young and beautiful as Elizabeth would be generally, and seldom censoriously, regarded as purchasable property. A stage beauty who *failed* to grace some aristocrat's bed, whether in or much more commonly and acceptably out of wedlock, might well be judged an oddity. These considerations become pertinent again in the next chapter of Elizabeth's adventures, where to the drama's cast-list the names must be added of two more principals, Captain Thomas Mathews, in the role of chief villain, and Richard Sheridan, hero.

Mathews had arrived in Bath with his wife at about the time of the Sheridans' coming there. He had earlier been an ensign in the army, but was generally known as 'Captain', perhaps from a commission in the militia, perhaps merely by courtesy. He was twenty-six, seven years married, Welsh, of good intelligence, an expert player of whist, popular, and well-to-do; and he seems to have enjoyed his reputation as a ladies' man. Well-known in Bath society, he had for some time been acquainted with the Linleys there. The suggestion that they might not have known he was married seems unrealistic, and of a piece with more of the legends and mutually incompatible accounts which multiplied around the story of the Sheridan-Linley romance.

What is beyond conjecture is that the amorous Mathews over several months pursued Elizabeth to the point of persecution; that Thomas Sheridan, his academy not flourishing, was off once again by mid-1771 to Dublin to stage a newly-completed comedy of his own, *Captain O'Blunder*; that the four young Sheridans, left behind in Bath, became close friends with the Linleys, who had now moved to fashionable Royal Crescent; that Elizabeth, not sufficiently sure of herself with her father and resisting seduction by Mathews, confided more and more in the Sheridan girls and their younger brother (Charles, the elder, left Bath to rid himself, so he declared, of his 'very ridiculous attachment' to Elizabeth, which was bringing him the 'pains' but not the 'sweets' of love); that finally between them they hatched a conspiracy, a plan of escape for the maiden in distress. The Sheridan girls had lived in France, and they had acquaintances there still living at St Quentin. Might not Elizabeth succeed in getting away from the importunities of Mathews by fleeing Bath for St Quentin?

For this desperate-sounding escapade an escort would be needed, and Sheridan, on the loose in Bath and ready for adventure, declared himself available. His attachment to Elizabeth, whether or not as 'ridiculous' as his brother's, was not yet avowed. His would be simply the role of a friend in time of necessity, a *cavaliere servente*, the protector of feminine honour – and indeed there is no cause to suppose it was otherwise. Many years later, at a time when his own amorous adventures were putting his relations with Elizabeth under serious strain, she (by then reproachfully) recalled:

> When I left Bath, I had not an idea of you but as a friend. It was not your person that gained my compassion. No, . . . it was that delicacy, that tender compassion, that interest which you seemed to take in my welfare, that were the motives which induced me to love you.

None of this, of course, need argue that he altogether failed to sense a hint of promise in the air. He was twenty, vigorous, and susceptible, she seventeen and dangerously attractive. It would not be long before they would be avowedly in love; but when it did happen, the force that drove them together came rather more passionately from her than from him.

Getting quietly away from Bath was the easiest part of the escapade. An evening was chosen when Thomas Linley would be engaged in his music away from home. Sheridan called for Elizabeth at Royal Crescent with a sedan chair to take her to a waiting post-chaise (and duenna or chaperon, by Alicia Lefanu's account) on the road to London, where they arrived the following day. At this point complications set in – and set in too for the reliability of the narration, for which alternative versions now multiply. (The chaperon, if there was one, soon disappears from the story.) All accounts agree that Sheridan managed to secure help from acquaintances in the City, in particular from John Ewart, 'a respectable brandy-merchant'. To Ewart he probably spun the yarn that Elizabeth was an heiress with whom he was eloping to wed in France. Through this London merchant, and with 'recommendations' from him to 'several persons at Lille', they obtained a passage for two on a vessel bound for Dunkirk.

The crossing however proved a nightmare, to Elizabeth especially, frail at the best of times, for they ran into a storm severe enough to give her a hatred of the sea for the rest of her life. From Dunkirk the battered travellers proceeded to Lille, the idea of going to St Quentin being abandoned; and at Lille Sheridan was able to get his charge accommodated as a boarder in a convent, where she was ill enough for a doctor to be called in. The convent was very likely a house of the Ursulines where the Prioress at this time was an Englishwoman. The doctor was an Englishman named Dolman who later took Elizabeth in at his own house.

Alicia Lefanu, Betsy Sheridan's daughter, wrote (half a century after the events) that on the way to Lille the couple were married 'at a village not far from Calais' by 'a priest who was known to be employed on such occasions'. This, Miss Lefanu claimed, was because, after the step she had taken, Elizabeth could not reappear in England 'but as his wife'. Most accounts of Sheridan have unquestioningly accepted this story, not unnaturally in view of the author's presumed inside knowledge; and indeed it is true that once, several months later, after Sheridan had called Mathews out in defence of his honour, Elizabeth did write to say that it was being 'strongly reported' that a marriage had taken place in France. Her father, she wrote to Sheridan, was reading her lectures 'with hopes that it is not true'. She was alleged to have disclosed the secret in her 'fright', calling out, 'My husband! My husband!' on being told of the second of his duels with Mathews. But some facts and circumstances sit uncomfortably with this part of Miss Lefanu's story. Elizabeth *was* soon reappearing in England and emphatically not as Sheridan's wife. Neither she nor Sheridan then acted or corresponded like a couple who regarded themselves as mutually pledged – and certainly no marriage at this time was consummated. (The law would of course have judged invalid any such ceremony as this 'at a village near Calais'; both parties were under age and the credentials of the 'priest' worse than suspect.) If either Thomas Sheridan or Thomas Linley entertained a suspicion that the marriage rumour was well founded, they at least had the prudence to show that they thought it was not. Again, it is difficult to reconcile the existence of any serious Calais ceremony with the tone and terms of Sheridan's anxiety expressed some months later when he heard talk that Elizabeth was to be married to Sir Thomas Clarges.

There was certainly no hint of marriage when, just four weeks after the flight from Bath, Sheridan wrote home to his brother Charles to explain what had happened and how things stood. He had written to Mathews; Elizabeth had been ill but was well again; *he* would soon be returning home; all his actions had of course been guided by 'honour and consistency'. But already on 9 April, six days before this, Mathews had 'posted' Sheridan in the *Bath Chronicle* for his 'scandalous method of running away from the place' and his 'insinuations' besmirching the reputations of both Mathews and Miss Linley. Sheridan in short was 'a L[iar] and a S[coundrel]'.

The gist of these public insults, to which the eighteenth-century gentleman could know only one honourable reply, was conveyed to Sheridan before he left Lille. Indeed, before he left, Thomas Linley had arrived there to reclaim his daughter. Linley appears to have taken her escapade, and Sheridan's part in it, in a most calm and businesslike manner. He even promised to allow Elizabeth to return to France, but only after she had fulfilled her engagements for which contracts were already signed. It was thus the three of them together who on 29 April journeyed homeward.

Sheridan had vowed that he would 'never sleep in England till he had thank'd Mathews as he deserved'. He went therefore immediately to find where Mathews was lodging in London, and tracked him down in Crutched Friars. However, the meeting there, late at night, Sheridan ostentatiously armed with pistols, proved rather an anticlimax. Mathews (by Sheridan's account) became all sweet reason and tried to divert blame on to Sheridan's brother Charles. But after Elizabeth, her father, and Sheridan arrived in Bath two days later, and Sheridan had found 'every one of Mathews's assertions totally and positively disavow'd' by Charles, he returned express to London, collected the brandy-merchant's son, Simon Ewart, to act as second, and called Mathews out. After traipsing rather ludicrously round Hyde Park and Covent Garden, Mathews objecting '*frequently* to the ground', they eventually fought inside the Castle Tavern at the corner of Bedford Street and Henrietta Street. Sheridan gained the advantage; Mathews, according to Sheridan, 'begged his life', but refused to deliver up his sword, whereupon Sheridan broke it 'and flung the hilt to the other end of the room'; and 'after much altercation' Mathews agreed to publish an apology for his *Bath Chronicle* paragraph in terms dictated by Sheridan. The argument might thus have been settled for good, had not Mathews harboured a grudge, which he was soon to convey to Bath's Master of Ceremonies, against Sheridan's breaches of duelling etiquette. Moreover he entertained a hope that he might one day contrive a return fixture. Meanwhile he left for Wales.

Thomas Sheridan now returned from Dublin, and although he could not exactly approve of his son's recent adventures – which incidentally involved him in settling the considerable debts incurred – and certainly would not favour a Sheridan-Linley marriage (Elizabeth's father, musician and carpenter's son, was clearly not a gentleman), yet he was not quite as emphatic as might have been expected. Perhaps this was partly because his soberer and more reliable son Charles helped to convince him that Sheridan had had to fight, 'otherwise he could never show his face'. Charles indeed (who was about to take up a very satisfactory and paternally approved post with the British embassy in Stockholm) wrote at this time to his uncle Richard, Sheridan's acting-guardian of Harrow days, that everything was 'concluded highly to the honour of Dick, who is applauded by everyone'.

Something deeper than applause came from Elizabeth. If she had not been in love with Sheridan before, she was now, and decidedly. Kept as much at a distance from him as possible by her father's orders, she was obliged to correspond in secret, and her letters vouch for the strength of her feeling. 'Oh my dearest love,' she wrote in May 1772, 'I am never happy but when I am with you. I cannot speak or think of anything else . . . I love you to distraction.' It was proving impossible to see him often, so he *must* write. She would prefer him and beggary to 'any other man and a throne . . . My hand shakes so at this moment I can scarce hold the pen. My father came into my room this moment, and I had just time to stuff the letter behind the glass.'

Although as 'Horatio' or 'Silvio' Sheridan sent pretty amatory verses to his 'Laura', he was in general, it is obvious, remiss in his replies to her:

> You unconscionable creature [she wrote] to make me sit up this time of the night to scribble nonsense to you, when you will not let me hear one word from you for this week to come. Oh my dear, you are the tyrant indeed . . . Why did you run away so soon tonight . . . My father . . . says he shall have a concert for my brother's benefit in a fortnight, and he shall expect my performance without any objections. You know I could not refuse him, but I am resolved never to go into public but on these occasions . . . Upon my knees, half naked [or as in fact she wrote, *half-nacked*], once more . . . I do insist that you write to me, you lazy wretch, can't you take so small a trouble . . . My sister is very impatient that I don't come into bed, but I feel more happiness in this situation, tho' I am half froze, than in the warmest bed in England.

Next month, June 1772, the Linleys took Elizabeth with them on a concert tour to Chester, Oxford, Cambridge, and other cities. She seized what she assured Sheridan was her very first opportunity to write, so busy she had been – and at night her mother had been taking away the candles. She longed to be back, to convince him how sincerely she was 'his Eliza', but nevertheless had to confess to 'perplexing thoughts'. Was he as constant to her as she to him? This was indeed a question which would obstinately persist throughout their twenty-year association.

Sheridan meanwhile had unfinished business to settle. When he 'refused to sign a paper testifying the spirit and propriety of

M's behaviour in the former rencounter', Mathews issued a challenge and a second duel had to be fought, this one on Kingsdown just outside Bath. In this contest *both* antagonists' swords were broken, but Mathews, grabbing the point end of his, gave Sheridan wounds severe enough for him to lie in some danger for a week. Mathews declared that his opponent's blood, with which the newspapers made copious play, was in fact vomited claret, Sheridan having arrived drunk. When recovered from the shock of learning of her hero's plight, Elizabeth, bound now for Wells, wrote to tell him once more that she did not know until that moment how much she loved him; and then added, just a little less convincingly: 'Believe me, had you died, I should certainly have dressed myself as a man and challenged M.'

It was from Wells that she wrote to him of rumours reporting that they had been secretly married in France. Thomas Sheridan and Thomas Linley, who seldom saw eye to eye, were agreed emphatically now on one matter. Linley could see no more virtue in a penniless claimant to his daughter's valuable hand than Sheridan senior in the daughter of a mere musician as a bride for his son. So, while Elizabeth was kept busy with further musical appearances (after the duels, naturally, she was more of a celebrity than ever), Sheridan was packed off to Waltham Abbey in Essex to study law. Mr Sheridan departed once more, this time with his daughters Lissy and Betsy, to Dublin.

During their enforced separation between August 1772 and April 1773, both Sheridan and Elizabeth passed through a sequence of shifting moods and contradictory resolves. In September he wrote to his friend Thomas Grenville (son of a past prime minister and brother to a future one):

But what shall I say of this attachment! To hope for happiness from it I must agree with you, 'is and *must* be impossible' – I have received a letter from her . . . fill'd with the violence of affection, and concluded with prayers, commands, and entreaties that I should write to her . . . If I consult my reason, or even one half of my feelings I find conviction that I should wish to end this unfortunate connexion – what draws the knot rejects the influence of reason.

The lovers had been forbidden to correspond, and *he* had determined not to. She continued to dodge her parents' vigilance and defied the ban. Throughout the autumn and spring of 1772–3 she was kept busy at her father's concerts, these culminating at Drury Lane during Lent, a season when the London theatres were given over to sacred oratorios. The applause and admiration Elizabeth then met with, Fanny Burney wrote, could 'only be compared with that given to Mr Garrick. The whole town seems distracted about her.' Honours were showered: first, a royal command performance, during which George III, that passionate Handelian, *ogled* Miss Linley (according to Horace Walpole) as much as he dared to 'in so holy a place as an oratorio'; then, at the Queen's (Buckingham) House, a five-hour marathon by the combined Linleys for the royal family alone, when the King, no bad judge of musical performance, declared to Mr Linley 'that he never in his life heard so fine a voice as his daughter's . . . she was a great credit to him' – and presented a bank note for £100.

Sheridan, away in Essex and spasmodically engaged upon the preliminary studies thought obligatory for a novice lawyer, did not remain altogether rusticated there. His letters to Grenville contain hints and allusions – intermingled with much portentous philosophizing upon Nature, the Passions, Woman, the Power of Virtue, et cetera – to social pleasures and urban amusements. Such references confirm that, however obstinately love for his lost Elizabeth recurs amid the high-flown periods, he was far from spending all his time repining over her in rural solitude. Once, three months after being exiled from Bath, sitting in the Bedford Street Coffee House (a favourite meeting-place for literary men) and 'being just come from the play', he suddenly felt the impulse to dash off to Grenville a few sentences of 'vile scrawl' which are a commentary upon his current way of life and state of mind:

[37]

Wherever I have been at an idle and irrational moment, whenever I have been in company with acquaintances and companions (that is with fools and coxcombs) I return with the strongest sensations of disgust, and I have no real friend on whom I can turn my thoughts, I am extremely wretched . . . Through this only I have taken a pen to scribble to *you*.

The principles of love are the same. – A lover (a true one) shall fly with rapture from the society of courtezans to contemplate but the picture of his mistress . . .

His mistress's picture of *him*, however, changed fast. Gossip found its way back to Bath and circulated merrily in that school for scandal. Suddenly Elizabeth's letters were on fire with resentment against the man who had used her 'so basely'.

I have been deceived [she wrote to him] by you and by everyone that it has almost deprived me of my reason, and I have paid too, too dear for my experience ever to put in your power or anyone's to impose on me again . . . When I tell you I have lately had some conversation with Mrs L. and Miss C—y, you will not suppose I will be again deceived.

Mrs L. and Miss C—y were presumably two ladies who shared in, or at least knew of, Sheridan's diversions.

On his side Sheridan expressed some bitterness too. Mathews, he heard, was still issuing calumnies against him in Bath. Moreover, so he wrote in sarcastic mood to Grenville, 'I find . . . that your friend Sir T. Clarges is either going to be married or to run away with Miss L.' Sir Thomas Clarges had indeed proposed marriage to Elizabeth before she left Bath for London. So too had 'other gentlemen of fortune'. But she had rejected them all with the same decisiveness as she had earlier, more questionable propositions. The state of siege she experienced was unrelenting. In London another suitor mounted the assault, and was being pressed by her father. 'He is not a young man,' she wrote to Sheridan, 'but I believe a worthy one.' (Further, he had promised

Linley that he would not touch Elizabeth's £3,000.) She could never *love* him, but – 'You see how I am situated. If this was not the case I could never be your wife, therefore once more I conjure you to leave me and cease persecuting me.' She begged him to return her letters or, if he would not, at least not to 'make an improper use of them. For God's sake write no more. I tremble at the consequences.'

It is at this point that the gap in the story yawns. Very shortly indeed after this, on 16 April 1773, the *Morning Chronicle* reported:

Tuesday was married at Marylebone Church by the Rev. Dr Booth the celebrated Miss Linley to Mr Sheridan. After the ceremony they set out with her family and friends, and dined at the Star and Garter on Richmond Hill; in the evening they had a ball after which the family and friends returned to town, and left the young couple at a gentleman's house in [Morden, near] Mitcham to consummate their nuptials.

The assumption must be that Linley and Sheridan had met; that Sheridan deployed all his formidable charm and – which was much to the point in dealing with Linley – offered favourable terms for Elizabeth: that is, he would consent to Linley's keeping a sizeable share of Elizabeth's fortune. By the terms of the marriage settlement of 10 April, £1,050 of Elizabeth's £3,000 was transferred 'to Swale and Linley in trust', the interest (the money was in 3 per cent Consols) to be paid 'to Mrs Sheridan for her life'. Perhaps, as Thomas Moore suggested in his biography of Sheridan, 'a series of stratagems and scenes' had convinced Linley 'that it was impossible much longer to keep his daughter and Sheridan asunder'. That may be a partial explanation, though it does sound like guesswork too.

Exactly one week before this sudden turn of events, no less happy for being largely unexplained, Sheridan the law student, with his father's approval and support, had been entered at the Middle Temple. Paternal approval, however, was emphatically

[39]

not what greeted news of the marriage. Dick had let him down, and let the family down. His sisters were forbidden to communicate with him, and his brother Charles was told, 'I consider myself now as having no son but you.'

Covent Garden
and The Rivals

THE long honeymoon was spent idyllically in
Buckinghamshire at East Burnham, a place compared with
which Paradise was but a kitchen garden – so Sheridan declared,
still luxuriating there a month after the wedding. Any thought of
further law studies was dismissed. He would soon try his hand, if
not very successfully, at a few literary and political articles for
newspapers and magazines; but for the time being he and his
Elizabeth* were content to exist – much more than exist, to bask –
in life's sunshine. They lived on Elizabeth's money, Sheridan,
twenty-two now, still being virtually penniless. However, their
'cottage' at East Burnham was, as Sheridan reported to
Grenville, 'a grand little mansion', and although they grew
'carrots and cabbages' in the gardens, conducted their household
'quite in the manner of plain mortals', and reckoned 'a gig and a
horse their only luxury', they were never without servants and
would soon be launching out in altogether grander style.

The fame Elizabeth Linley had won as a singer meant that she
was still in heavy demand for concerts, and some of the offers now
made to her were dazzling – £3,000, for instance, for a sequence

---

* Sheridan's favourite name for his first wife was Betsy or, as he usually spelt it,
Betsey. To many of her friends and relations she was Eliza. Here she will be
Elizabeth or Mrs Sheridan, but not Betsy. To avoid confusion, that name is
reserved for Sheridan's younger sister, later Mrs Henry Lefanu.

of twenty appearances in oratorio. But Sheridan, except for two very special occasions, forbade all such public engagements. A gentleman's wife must not sing in public for payment; and Sheridan, who retained unpleasant memories of being the player's son, had no intention of becoming merely the singer's husband. It was only when pressure was put on him by Convocation at Oxford and by the Three Choirs Festival committee at Worcester (where her 100-guinea fee was donated to charity) that he permitted his wife those two final appearances, and then only because they were engagements for which her father had earlier contracted.

This independence of spirit, this apparent self-denial, by one who was far from denying the advantages attaching to money has been sometimes ascribed, then and since, to false pride or merely snobbery; but one century's false pride is another's course of honour, one era's snobbery another's propriety. Sheridan's motives are plain. His status as a gentleman being insecure, he was determined to secure it; and it is of interest to find, among those supporting the stand he took, another who had his own reasons for being sensitive in this area. When a member of the company in conversation one day with Dr Johnson at Mr Cambridge's Twickenham villa criticized Sheridan's firmness in refusing Thomas Linley his daughter's continued services, Johnson's view was no less decided than was usual with him. Sheridan had 'resolved nobly and wisely to be sure. He is a brave man. Would a gentleman not be disgraced by having his wife sing publicly for hire?' Johnson was ready to go further: 'public practice of any art, and staring in men's faces' was, he observed, 'very indelicate in a female'.

Among the offers turned down on his wife's behalf by Sheridan in 1774 was one from the King, made through John Stanley who was manager for the Lent oratorios at Covent Garden, for Mrs Sheridan to continue in them under royal patronage. 'I should imagine Mr Stanley would apply to you,' Sheridan wrote to his father-in-law; 'I said you had twenty Mrs Sheridans more.' However, it was not Sheridan's intention to let his wife's talent run to waste. Early in 1774 he took a lease of No 28 Orchard Street, fashionably placed near Portman Square, and was soon using the newly adapted music-room there for private concerts for his invited guests from among the nobility and gentry. Thomas Linley helped to furnish and equip this new home, a measure of the good relations now established between him and Sheridan.

Return invitations to musical parties came from, among others, the Earl of Coventry and Sir Joshua Reynolds, whom Sheridan offended at first by taking umbrage at the suggestion that his wife was 'to sing for her supper'. It was shortly after this that Reynolds painted 'Mrs Sheridan as St Cecilia'; but, soulfully as his rapt Cecilia gazes, as a representation of a real-life Mrs Sheridan his portrait falls short of the two elegant canvases by Gainsborough painted at Bath some years before. (One of them is the appealing 'fancy picture' showing her and her brother Tom as 'a beggar boy and girl'; the other depicts her standing beside her sister Mary.) Beauty she had; health she had not. More than once during these early years of marriage Thomas Linley felt the need to warn Sheridan of her vulnerability. At Bath they were 'all in great anxiety about her' in the November after the April wedding, and six months later, after a second miscarriage, Linley wrote of his daughter's 'seminal weakness'. 'You must absolutely keep from her,' he urged, very alarmingly, 'for every time you touch her, you drive a nail into her coffin.' However, there then followed a successful pregnancy, and by November 1775 everyone was rejoicing in the birth of a son, yet another Thomas.

That same month a new play was in the hands of the Covent Garden manager, ready for rehearsal. Sheridan's energies had not been restricted to organizing fashionable private entertainment. He had made useful contacts with the men who controlled London's public music-making and theatre-going, Thomas Harris of Covent Garden among them – to whom he had put forward the latest product of his pen. From writing on topical controversies he had turned hopefully towards writing for the theatre.

[43]

Among his mother's comedies was one, possibly never finished, called *A Journey* (or *A Trip*) *to Bath*. There is some evidence that Garrick had read it and rejected it. Thomas Sheridan after his wife's death had given this play, or what his daughter Betsy called the 'sketch' of it, to Sheridan before the family left Bath, and it is possible that Sheridan had had a shot at improving or adapting it at some stage before 1774. It contains among its characters a Mrs Tryfort whose foreshadowing of Mrs Malaprop is unmistakable, even to her 'progeny of learning' and 'contagious countries' – though whether these particular felicities originated with Frances Sheridan or her son there is no means of knowing. In any case the idea behind Mrs Tryfort-Malaprop, the outrageous near-miss, predates both Sheridans by centuries, and there has never been any credible suggestion that *The Rivals* was to any significant degree plagiarized; this despite similarities between parts of it and of certain comedies by Sheridan's near-contemporaries Colman, Murphy, and Garrick. Undeniably also there are strokes in it which have precursors in Restoration comedy: Bob Acres' 'sentimental swearing', for instance ('Odds levels and aims!' 'Odds hilts and blades!') does seem to derive directly from Wittol in Congreve's *Old Bachelor*, where we find 'Gad's daggers, belts, blades, and scabbards!' etc. None of this adds up to very much; a similar game may be played with several of the plays of Shakespeare. However, Sheridan's awareness that a charge of plagiarism might be levelled is indicated by his not quite credible assertion in the play's preface that as a tyro he had deliberately avoided reading earlier plays, so that his 'invention' might not be 'impaired by his recollection'.

The Rivals was staged at Covent Garden on 17 January 1775. It was not a success. It was much too long; some of the players were not word-perfect; and strong exception was taken both to the character Sheridan had written into Sir Lucius O'Trigger and to the manner in which the actor John Lee had played him. The reviewer from the *Morning Post* had never before seen 'so villanous a portrait of an Irish gentleman permitted so openly to insult that country,' and the *Morning Chronicle* wrote of 'an affront to the common sense of an audience'. The play was withdrawn after the first night.

Sheridan never easily accepted defeat. He immediately set about making cuts and removing what he called 'excrescences'; recasting passages which had made the first-night audience restive; transforming Sir Lucius O'Trigger from an undignified fortune-hunter into a proud if impecunious Irish gentleman with some of the best lines in the play; persuading the Covent Garden manager to give it another chance. For Sir Lucius there was to be a change of actors, the much abused John Lee giving way to Lawrence Clinch, who was to make so pronounced a success in the part that Sheridan wrote his next play, the short farce *St Patrick's Day or the Scheming Lieutenant*, as a vehicle for Clinch on his benefit night.

The Rivals was ready for its second performance only eleven days after its first, and ran for fifteen nights – a good showing for those days. A favourable reception for it followed at Bath, and since then it has been one of the most regularly revived of English comedies. Perhaps a factor, if only a minor one, in its initial success was the faintly autobiographical flavour audiences thought they detected in it, topical parallels between the dialogue and action of the play and the adventures of the author and his wife. It is hardly to be supposed that a public so recently treated to the scandals of *The Maid of Bath* and to newspaper coverage of the fortunes of Miss Linley and Richard Sheridan should fail to sense a piquant relevance in such lines as these of the heroine, Lydia Languish, when she has been baulked of her longed-for romance:

Why, is it not provoking? when I thought we were coming to the prettiest distress imaginable, to find myself made a mere Smithfield bargain at last! There, had I projected one of the most sentimental elopements! so becoming a disguise! – so amiable a ladder of ropes! Conscious moon – four horses – Scotch parson – . . . and such paragraphs in the newspapers! – Oh, I shall die with disappointment!

Or in such sentiments as those of the hero, Captain Absolute: 'Can a man commit a more heinous offence against another than to fall in love with the same woman?' The action of *The Rivals* was all located in Bath; part of its plot revolves round duelling, though it is duelling as burlesque; and even the comedy's title might suggest the well publicized rivalry between Mathews and Sheridan. It is unlikely that he was unaware of such half-hinted allusions or was above making theatrical capital out of the notoriety that had come unbidden to him and his Elizabeth.

The Rivals' fifteen-night run was soon to be eclipsed by Sheridan's first really big success – a seventy-five-night run for his comic opera, *The Duenna*: longer even, by thirteen performances, than that of *The Beggar's Opera* half a century earlier, and with many revivals to come in the half-century to follow. The music for this production, 'a comedy of action in the Spanish style', was by both Thomas Linleys, father and son, and in the fitting of music to text the rapport by post between Sheridan in London and his father-in-law in Bath proved excellent. The 'we' in Sheridan's side of the correspondence moreover shows clearly that his wife (then very near to the birth of their child) provided a fourth member of the team, as musical adviser to the author. Through the autumn of 1775 there was an urgent flow of suggestions and counter-suggestions and emendations: could Linley provide an oboe obbligato at this point, 'to cut a figure' and provide a passionate passage at that, to give Miss Brown the opportunity 'to show in it as much execution as she is capable of, which is pretty well'? And then: 'Unless you can give us three days in town, I fear our opera will stand a chance to be ruined.' As it turned out, Miss Brown, *The Duenna's* Donna Clara, was to execute 'a passionate passage' of a different nature after the show had been running for a week or two. Quite in the spirit of the author's personal history and of the opera's sub-title (*The Duenna or The Double Elopement*) she herself eloped twice, first unavailingly but then successfully. The production however sailed triumphantly through such buffetings and ended by making useful money for the author. This was a new experience, coming the more pleasurably to one who until that time had been uncomfortably dependent on his wife's financing.

The style of *The Rivals*, 'the comedy of character', had been in direct descent from Restoration comedy, but in a Georgian, which is to say vastly more respectable, idiom. (Sheridan was firm on respectability: when preparing *The Duenna* he wrote to Linley, 'We dare not propose a peep beyond the ancles on any account; for the critics in the pit at a new play are much greater prudes than the ladies in the boxes.') *The Duenna* too had a long pedigree – the tradition of 'the comedy of action', more particularly in a setting of Spanish intrigue: what Dryden called simply 'the Spanish plot'. Spanish on the surface as *The Duenna* was, like *The Rivals* it still managed to contain many innuendos harking back to the author's own adventures.

The Beggar's Opera has survived on stage for two and a half centuries, both in its own clothes and those later provided by Brecht and Weill. *The Duenna* has failed to last similarly, yet its libretto reads a good deal better than that of most light operas, and the music, in view of its provenance, must surely have quality. An opera which is never heard* or seen cannot be fairly judged; but it is interesting that among the critics of Sheridan's own day, two of the best, who had seen it, Johnson and Hazlitt, both rated it very highly indeed. Proposing Sheridan for The Literary Club, Johnson said, 'He who has written the two best comedies of the age is surely a considerable man' – and he meant *The Rivals* and *The Duenna*, the first performance of *The School for Scandal* being at that time still two months away. Hazlitt's verdict was stronger still:

> The Duenna is a perfect work of art. It has the utmost sweetness and point. The plot, the characters, the dialogue, are all complete in themselves, and they are all his own; and the songs are the best that ever were written, except those in the Beggar's Opera.

---

* It *has* been revived, very rarely, in this century, once at the Lyric Theatre Hammersmith in the 1920s, and once, much updated, at Bristol in the 1980s.

Thomas Moore called it, quite simply, 'the best opera in the language'.

The Rivals, *St Patrick's Day*, and *The Duenna* were all Covent Garden productions, under the Harris management. Covent Garden's only serious rival was the other Theatre Royal, in Drury Lane. These were the only two playhouses holding a patent under the statute of 1737 for the main season that ran from September to June. Of the two other London houses at this time, both in the Haymarket, one, the King's Theatre, was licensed only for French or Italian opera, and the other, the Little Theatre, only for the short summer season. Thus although there always lingered a fear that a third playhouse would be granted the royal patent, for the greater part of the year Covent Garden and Drury Lane between them monopolized the London stage.

At Drury Lane Garrick still reigned, as he had for the past twenty-eight years; but now he was fifty-eight, thinking of retirement, and casting round for a dependable successor. Drury Lane's value was assessed at £70,000, of which his own share was one half, the other half belonging to one Willoughby Lacy, who was unwilling to part with it. At first Garrick approached the playwright and theatrical manager George Colman the elder, who proved to be uninterested unless he could be offered purchase of the whole. (Colman, the nephew of Lord Bath, was a man of means.) Impressed by the showing that young Sheridan was making at the rival house, where indeed *The Duenna* was providing uncomfortably strong competition, Garrick next turned confidentially in that direction. It was December 1775; Sheridan was only a few weeks into his *Duenna* triumph and still far from being a rich man, but the prospect fired him. Dick was likely to 'fall into a bustling life', his mother had once predicted, so he must learn to 'shift for himself'. This he now proceeded to do with the utmost energy and enthusiasm, bustling away for the next month or more, in secret of course, contacting lawyers, approaching likely partners, searching out possible mortgagees, negotiating with Garrick, who happily – so Sheridan reported to his father-in-law – seemed 'likely always to continue our friend'.

David Garrick, painted here by Thomas Gainsborough, was the most brilliant actor of his day, and was manager and part-owner of Drury Lane theatre.

[49]

Obviously Thomas Linley, who had had his eye on opportunities at Drury Lane before, was one potential partner. Another
was John Ewart, the 'respectable brandy merchant' and earlier
friend in need during the flight with Elizabeth to France. Dr
James Ford, a wealthy physician and fashionable man-midwife,
made a third. Sheridan moreover had hopes of enlisting into the
enterprise his own father who was back on the London stage
again after a lapse of sixteen years, at Drury Lane itself, in
another revival of Addison's perennial *Cato*. 'My father offers his
services on our own terms,' Sheridan wrote optimistically to his
father-in-law. On a personal level, readmittance to his father's
approval was likely to bring not only a salve to old wounds, but
the lifting of the paternal interdict on meeting his sisters Lissy
and Betsy. It was now nearly three years since they had been
allowed to see him, though once during the run of *The Rivals* he
did experience the melancholy pleasure of seeing *them* from the
wings enjoying his comedy from one of the boxes. The
complicated bargaining and negotiating could hardly stay secret
long, and he was very aware of the awkwardness of his current
obligation to Covent Garden. As he told his father-in-law, they
must be determined and they must be speedy. 'You are such a
sanguine pig,' his wife wrote to him once, and sanguine he
certainly was of his prospects now. The annual interest on Drury
Lane, he informed Linley on New Year's Eve, was £3,500 – that
is 5 per cent; 'while this is *cleared* the proprietors are *safe* – but I
think it must be *infernal* management indeed that does not double
it'. Four days later, after seeing in rough Garrick's accounts for
the past seven years, he *had* doubled it: 'Valuing the property at
£70,000,' he blithely wrote, 'the interest has exceeded ten per
cent.'

John Ewart withdrew from the proposed partnership, but Dr
Ford agreed to increase his share, so that the required £35,000
was divided eventually between Linley (£10,000), Sheridan
(£10,000) and Ford (£15,000). Linley's share was raised largely
through a mortgage on his property in Bath, the mortgagee being
Garrick himself. Sheridan's share came from £1,300 of his own

[50]

and his wife's, with the remainder through Dr Ford and Garrick's lawyers – though so bald a statement cuts through labyrinthine complications. Dr Ford thus emerged as the principal capitalist behind Sheridan's grand enterprise in its original half-share form – which brought forth a few smiles. The actress Kitty Clive, for instance, Garrick's partner in past Drury Lane comedies, wrote to him: 'What a strange jumble of people they have put in the papers as the purchasers of the patent! I thought I should have died laughing when I saw a man-midwife among them: I suppose they have taken him in to prevent *miscarriages!*' But resolutely Sheridan put aside the possibility of such misfortunes, and was soon rallying Linley because he dealt 'in apprehension by the pound' while only taking 'confidence by the grain'.

In the new firm, which was a going concern from June 1776, Linley was musical director and Thomas Sheridan the proposed stage director, which last signalled a short period of at least somewhat improved relations between father and son; short, since the father soon took umbrage and left once more for Dublin when the son refused him permission to act. Had not the departure of Garrick ('whose jealousy had long shut the London theatres against me') offered Thomas a chance, as he put it, to *retrieve his affairs?* It was 'merely to gratify' his son, he protested, that he grudgingly acquiesced in the terms offered, but his 'worst enemy . . . determined upon ruining' him and his family could hardly have treated him worse. The terms offered, second time round, in 1778, specifically excluded stage appearances. Four years later Thomas Sheridan left his son's theatre for good.

Thus, with Garrick's approval and influence behind him, Sheridan effectively became Drury Lane manager at the age of twenty-four. But at first he was not quite unquestioned master there, for there still remained the other half-share; and when its owner Willoughby Lacy proposed introducing two of his associates into the team of proprietors, battle had to be joined to ensure Sheridan's managerial control. On his side, fortunately for him, were most of the theatre's actors and actresses, among whom a pro-Sheridan demonstration in the form of a boycott of rehearsals almost brought business to a standstill in October 1776. Sheridan, as confident of success as ever, wrote in amused approval to Garrick:

> Indeed there was never known such an uncommonly epidemick disorder as has raged among our unfortunate company – it differs from the plague by attacking the better sort first – the manner too in which they are seiz'd I am told is very extraordinary – many who were in perfect health at one moment, on receiving a billet from the prompter to summon them to their business are seiz'd with sudden qualms . . .

No longer under challenge as sole manager after that autumn, Sheridan was still not satisfied. By means of financial moves as complicated as they were ambitious, he greatly increased his proportion of the Drury Lane proprietorship by taking over Lacy's mortgaged half-share, at a price of £10,000 over the £35,000 at which it had first been valued, while selling his own original £10,000, half to Linley, and half to Ford. He was obliged however to bind himself in two annuities of £500 each to guarantee his mortage interest payments – a burden destined to prove uncommonly strict, with lateness in payments almost leading at one point to a break with Garrick. Even now not satisfied, by 1780 he had bought out Dr Ford too, so that except for Linley's share he succeeded in becoming, as well as sole manager, sole proprietor too. All these intricate deals were completed without any disbursement of cash beyond the £1,300 contributed as down-payment for his first 1776 mortgage. Such an apparent triumph of financial legerdemain becomes a little easier to understand when it is remembered that the security for all these tangled loans and mortgages was Drury Lane itself, whose value, already £70,000 in 1775, was rising steeply through the following decade.

Rising also were its owner's ambitions, and with them his personal expenditure. His tendencies always inclined towards those professed by old Sir Oliver in *The School for Scandal*: 'Sir, when I take a whim in my head I don't value money.' Soon after acquiring Drury Lane he left Orchard Street for a better house in Great Queen Street, which he afterwards continued to maintain when taking a still more fashionable one in Grosvenor Place. Then by the summer of 1779 he was in occupation of a large house at Heston in Middlesex, and kept it for two years. A passion, almost a mania, for houses, and with it a compulsion to be forever on the move, would never leave him.

By now the Sheridans had been accepted into the 'best' society. For a time it was still Mrs Sheridan who enjoyed a priority of attention, as when Fanny Burney, after meeting them both for the first time, rhapsodized over her captivating elegance and beauty, her 'look of ease and happiness', her complete absence of 'airs of any kind'. Sheridan too came in for Miss Burney's firm if supplementary approval: fine figure, face good but not handsome, upright, manly, fashionable 'without the smallest tincture of foppery or modish graces . . . every way worthy his beautiful companion'. The only woman to rival her for beauty, Miss Burney thought, was Mrs Crewe, and it so happened that Frances Anne Crewe, Fulke Greville's daughter, was for a time now to figure as the first of those fashionable great ladies with whom Sheridan habitually aspired to philander. Indeed it was as 'Philander' that he portrayed himself in the verses he was soon writing in honour of this 'Amoret' with the 'all-conquering eyes'. Some were later published in the form of a dedication *Address'd to a Lady with the Comedy of the School for Scandal* ('. . . my Inspirer and my Model, CREWE!').

Others besides Sheridan composed verses in praise of 'Amoret' – Charles Fox for one and even Elizabeth Sheridan for another. Indeed she it was, perhaps, who invented the name. Both Sheridans were on friendly terms with Mrs Crewe for at least ten years, so that suggestions of a secret relationship seem implausible. That, however, does not mean that Mrs Sheridan was able to banish from her heart all jealousy. Once, for instance, when she was away in Bath with her parents and he wrote her an

The beautiful Mrs Crewe was one of the fashionable great ladies with whom Sheridan flirted, calling her 'Amoret' in his verses. Mezzotint after the portrait by D. Gardner.

enthusiastic account, together with verses in her own praise, of a glittering function he had attended in intimate company with some of the *beau monde*'s queens of fashion – the Duchesses of Devonshire and Rutland, Mrs Crewe, Lady Jersey, Lady Craven, Lady Granby – she replied in kind (her facility in light verse was more than adequate, and here ran to thirty stanzas), praying that his heart might stay faithful and 'beat for her alone'. There was no serious rift yet between them – but she could hardly be altogether blind to the evidences of his roving eye, or fail to see how his vanity was tickled by the attention such celebrated beauties and grand ladies seemed anxious to pay him.

The School for Scandal
and The Critic

DRURY LANE'S first few months under Sheridan were not
particularly auspicious. A 'young gentlewoman' Mary
Robinson, coached by Garrick, made her stage début as Juliet,
though it was her later appearance in *The Winter's Tale* that
attached to her, permanently, the name of Perdita and, very
temporarily, the ardent attentions of the young Prince of Wales.
Thomas Linley junior wrote the music and Philippe de
Loutherbourg produced the stage designs and scenic effects for a
'dramatic romance', the part of whose heroine was taken by Mrs
Baddeley. Three of Congreve's best-known comedies were
revived with anything too risqué removed or adapted. Hence
when Mr Dangle later in *The Critic* (1779) referred to 'even
Congreve and Vanbrugh' being 'obliged to undergo a bungling
reformation', it was one of Sheridan's jokes against his own
practices. The best known of all such reformations, whether
bungling or not, was the new manager's rewriting of Vanbrugh's
The Relapse, or Virtue in Danger, first staged at Drury Lane in
1696 just before the reaction set in against Restoration bawdy. In
Sheridan's version the danger to Amanda's virtue was made
rather less peremptory. Berinthia was no longer borne offstage by
Loveless crying (but *diminuendo*, or as Vanbrugh had saucily
directed, 'very softly'), 'Help, help! I'm ravished, ruined,
undone.' A suggestion of homosexuality was expunged by the

expedient of substituting an old woman's part for a man's, and there were other such shifts towards the propriety demanded by mid-Georgian convention. But basically *The Trip to Scarborough*, as Sheridan renamed it, remained Vanbrugh's *The Relapse*. The reception it had in its new guise was unpromising. At one point, Berinthia, in the person of Mrs Yates (whose real forte was tragedy) was hissed off the stage, leaving Mrs Robinson as Amanda in precarious occupation of it, sustained however by the Duke of Cumberland's encouragement from the stage-box and Sheridan's exhortations from the wings.

A good new comedy was demanded, and Sheridan set to work to assemble one from various earlier ideas of his own – sketches, jottings, characters, situations, which existed until then only as discrete fragments. The first performance was due on 8 May 1777, and until the very last moment Sheridan was adding, revising, re-polishing, to the frustration and even exasperation of actors and auxiliaries alike. As the ink of the last full stop dried (it was more likely to have been a dash than a full stop; Sheridan's punctuation, more eccentric even than his spelling, luxuriated in dashes), he wrote underneath, 'Finished at last, thank God, R.B. Sheridan', to which the prompter appended his own heartfelt 'Amen, W. Hopkins'. The play, of course, was *The School for Scandal*.

A last-minute hitch was overcome after the piece had initially been refused a performing licence. Certain of its topical references had appeared to be aimed against the Court candidate then fighting John Wilkes in the election for City Chamberlain, and in particular against moneylending practices which were judged to be too closely akin to those of the new comedy's 'honest Israelite', Moses. But when Sheridan was able to see the Licenser, Lord Hertford, in person, objection was removed.

Although Sheridan's Congreve revivals had received poor box-office support, the casting and acting of them by his company had reaped high praise. Now their performance in *The School for Scandal* was universally acclaimed. 'To my great astonishment,' wrote Horace Walpole, 'there were more parts

performed admirably . . . than I almost ever saw in any play . . .
It seemed a marvellous resurrection of the stage.' Indeed several
of the comedy's characters had been created in view of the
peculiar talents of individual actors and actresses. Thomas King,
who had been Sir Anthony Absolute in *The Rivals* and was soon
to be Mr Puff in *The Critic*, played Sir Peter Teazle. Lady Teazle
was Mrs Abington, Drury Lane's leading lady, who had once
sold flowers in the street but was currently the mistress of the
future Prime Minister, Lord Shelburne.* A pattern of high
fashion and polished manners, she was admirably suited, though
she was now approaching forty, to the role of the pert and pretty
young wife from the country dangerously attracted by London's
sophistication, expensive living, scandalmongering, and extra-
marital adventure – but of course, this being not Restoration
comedy but Sheridan, rescued finally from this last (if only by the
merest chance) and restored to the loving arms of that decent old
stick, her husband. Mrs Abington had recently played the
husband-hungry country wench in *The Trip to Scarborough*
(Miss Hoyden) and been Lydia Languish in *The Rivals* earlier.
Charles Surface, dissipated but generous-hearted, the young
rake with the heart of gold who some thought was modelled on
Charles Fox, others on Sheridan himself, was played by William
'Gentleman' Smith, once of Eton and King's, whose departure
from Cambridge had been brought about, aptly enough, through
'a little extravagance which deranged his finances' and 'an
unlucky elevation caused by liquor'. Charles's sententious,
hypocritical brother Joseph, Lady Teazle's would-be seducer,
was John Palmer, previously Jack Absolute in *The Rivals* and
then Sneer in *The Critic*. He was said to *be* Joseph Surface, 'at
least in his polished and plausible manners . . . and his winning

---

* Her connection with Shelburne, who allowed her £50 a week and a house in
Piccadilly, had only four months previously been advertised to the world, under
transparent disguises, in one of those bedroom-keyhole revelations which were
the speciality of London's two chief journalistic purveyors of tittle-tattle, the
Town and Country Magazine and the *Morning Post*. Scandal-sheets like these
(the first of them mentioned by name) were of course among the targets of *The
School for Scandal*'s satire.

way of making insincere apologies'. Similarly, at least by her fellow players, Miss Pope was alleged to be Mrs Candour, the scandalmonger. The Sir Benjamin Backbite was played by J.W. Dodd, already with a high reputation for portraying oddities, butts, and fops; he had been Bob Acres in *The Rivals* and Lord Foppington in *The Trip to Scarborough*. Even Trip, the footman, was played by someone of whom it was said that 'the gentleman's gentleman fitted him like his clothes', the mincing, drawling, and extremely elegant Mr La Mash. For the *ingénue* part of Maria, Sheridan had intended Mary Robinson, but pregnancy having as she put it 'unshaped' her, she was obliged to withdraw.

The new play delighted its first-night audience, and *almost* perfectly satisfied the reviewers. Horace Walpole, seeing it a month or two later, wrote, 'I have seen no comedy that comes near it since Vanbrugh's *The Provoked Husband*.' Since then, there have not been many critics to dissent from the opinion that Sheridan had written the best comedy of manners, or 'artificial' comedy, in the language. Of earlier plays, perhaps Congreve's *Way of the World*, and of later, probably only Oscar Wilde's *The Importance of Being Earnest* would present a widely supported challenge for that pride of place. The dialogue sparkles unfailingly. The intricate, but not over-intricate, plot is managed most expertly. The sentiment never gets out of hand – indeed an important strand in the plot is the exposure and disgrace of the man of false sentiment. The cynicism which sometimes imbues Restoration comedy is absent, unless it be thought a kind of cynicism to contrive that Lady Teazle escapes adultery by the merest accident. Any accusation of substantial plagiarism (in particular from Arthur Murphy's almost contemporary *Know Your Own Mind*, with which there are undoubted similarities) hardly stands up against the evidence of Sheridan's own much earlier fragmentary drafts and sketches. All in all, it is hard to think of another play which more satisfyingly balances dialogue and action, situation and characterization, wit and sentiment, satire and gaiety, delicate humour and telling ridicule. As for the famous screen scene, it has been said that as a detachable unit of its own it constitutes the best one-act play in the language. It proved a sensation on the first night, with a spontaneous outburst of 'prolonged, violent, and tumultuous applause' at the artfully delayed *coup de théâtre* when the screen is at last thrown down and Lady Teazle stands discovered.

The 1776–7 Drury Lane season at least ended prosperously with the success of *The School for Scandal*. The accounts, neatly and efficiently kept by Mrs Sheridan, show it consistently heading the box-office takings. However, the 1777–8 season went badly. Garrick was pessimistic that his 'poor old Drury' would 'soon be in the hands of the Philistines'. Sheridan contributed nothing new that year, but shortly after the start of the 1778–9 season he was ready with a hastily written reach-me-down topical entertainment, with music by Linley and spectacle by de Loutherbourg. It was a time when any crisis facing Drury Lane was dwarfed by the one facing the whole nation. France had allied with Britain's American rebels, and there was fear of a French invasion. The fleet was on full alert, and southern England was patriotically busy with drilling militiamen and military exercises. Even the Whigs, who had been strongly critical of the Lord North government and often sympathetic to the rebels so long as hostilities were confined to America, were now as belligerent as any against the French; and while the young male aristocrats donned uniform and supervised parades, their ladies (the Duchess of Devonshire among them) adopted 'military' fashions of their own and indulged the modish whim of camping out amid *fête-champêtre* luxury next to the main anti-invasion headquarters camp at Coxheath near Maidstone.

It was long thought that *The Camp* was not by Sheridan at all, but by his close friend Richard Tickell, the husband of Mrs Sheridan's sister Mary. It seems however that although this little two-act 'entertainment' was very much a co-operative venture, its text was at least largely, and perhaps mainly, by Sheridan. Written at speed, it served its ephemeral purpose well, running for sixty-eight performances and nicely catching the patriotic theatre-going mood of 1778. However, in the words of one of the

The famous screen scene from the original production of Sheridan's 'The School for Scandal', painted by James Roberts. From left to right: Thomas King as Sir Peter Teazle, Mrs Abington as Lady Teazle, William Smith as Charles Surface, and John Palmer as Joseph Surface.

reviews, 'the writer and the composer are so totally eclipsed by the painter that the entertainment of *The Camp* will always be attributed to the talents of Mr de Loutherbourg.' The eye-catching and money-spinning impact of this brilliant artist's ingenious scenic effects was not lost upon either Sheridan or Sheridan's immortal creation of the following season, Mr Puff in *The Critic*. 'Now, gentleman,' explains Puff, 'this scene goes entirely for what we call SITUATION or STAGE EFFECT, by which the greatest applause may be obtained, without the assistance of language, sentiment, or character.' And in the finale of *The Critic* Mr Sheridan-Puff was to give both the excellent de Loutherbourg and Linley's chorus all the scope they could have desired, in a grand nautical patriotic spectacle which the *London Evening Post* found 'truly picturesque' and the public loved:

Flourish of drums – trumpets – cannon, etc. etc. Scene changes to the sea – the fleets engage – the musick plays 'Britons strike home' – Spanish fleet destroyed by fireships, etc. – English fleet advances – musick plays 'Rule Britannia' – the procession of all the English rivers and their tributaries with their emblems, etc. begins with Handel's water musick – ends with a chorus, to the march in Judas Maccabeus.

Primarily, of course, *The Critic, or a Tragedy Rehearsed*, first played on 30 October 1779 as an after-piece to the evening's main fare, *Hamlet*, was not a de Loutherbourg spectacular. Like *The Camp* it was for the most part an 'entertainment', but infinitely funnier, wittier, more farcical, more satirical. It had something for everybody. The opening scene, which Sheridan considered, and rightly, the best he ever wrote, was in the sharpest *School for Scandal* manner: ridicule of 'jobbing critics' and 'lackeys of literature', fun at the expense of newspaper gossip and theatrical tittle-tattle, and light-hearted demolition of the vanity of Sir Fretful Plagiary, a creation whom the audience found no difficulty in identifying with the contemporary tragedian Richard Cumberland. The actor playing the part, William

[62]

Parsons, to underline the point even chose to affect a well-known idiosyncrasy in Cumberland's style of dress. Sheridan presumably thought Cumberland to be fair game: one of the best-known, though maybe apocryphal, Sheridan anecdotes relates how Cumberland, taking his children to see *The School for Scandal*, reproved them for laughing too freely at it – 'keep still, you little dunces, there is nothing to laugh at!' – which being reported to him, Sheridan remarked that he saw no reason why Cumberland should not laugh at his comedy since *he* had laughed a great deal at Cumberland's recently staged tragedy.

Sheridan stopped short of making his Cumberland-Plagiary character the author of the 'historical tragedy' whose parody of a 'rehearsal' by the richly preposterous Mr Puff, its author-producer, provides the main substance of the burlesque – with the consequence that *The Critic* almost becomes two plays, with Sir Fretful disappearing after the brilliant first scene, leaving from Scene One only Messrs Dangle and Sneer to be conducted with the audience through the hilarities of Mr Puff's tragedy.

It is surprising that a satirical burlesque like *The Critic*, abounding in topical references and in-jokes, can still hold the stage, and even the television screen, so successfully. In fact its television showing in 1982 with Alan Badel as Sir Fretful, and Hywel Bennett as Mr Puff, made excellent viewing. It had moreover the effrontery – quite in Sheridan's vein – to employ Sir John Gielgud to play the wordless part of Lord Burleigh, intended to guy the then Prime Minister Lord North, who comes on stage merely to sit down, *think*, shake his head, and depart. 'Such interesting gravity,' Mr Puff comments; was it likely 'that a Minister in his situation, with the whole affairs of the nation in his head, should have time to talk'?

Although *The Critic*'s inventive absurdities and shafts of good-natured satire have enough fun and high spirits for them to survive and flourish after two centuries, for Sheridan and his players and the habitués of Drury Lane they had much of the nature of a family game. Thomas King, for instance, acting the part of the 'practitioner of panegyric' Mr Puff, and quoting from an imaginary critique, was made to refer to fellow-actors on stage, *and to himself*, as follows:

> . . . Characters strongly drawn – highly coloured – hand of a master – fund of genuine humour – mine of invention – neat dialogue – attic salt! Then for the performance – MR DODD [who was acting Dangle] was astonishingly great in the character of SIR HARRY! That universal and judicious actor MR PALMER [playing Sneer] perhaps never appeared to more advantage than in the COLONEL – but it is not in the power of language to do justice to MR KING! Indeed he more than merited those repeated bursts of applause which he drew from a brilliant and judicious audience.

There was a good deal more of this domestic Drury Lane fun. The prompter William Hopkins appeared as a member of the cast. There was mention of Fosbrook, the theatre treasurer. When the heroine of Mr Puff's tragedy, Tilburina, appeared ('stark mad in white satin . . . according to custom' with her confidante mad also, 'in white linen'), the actress playing her was giving an easily recognizable impersonation of a leading tragedy actress of the day, Ann Barry (Mrs Crawford). And Sheridan slyly makes Sir Fretful Plagiary, explaining why his new tragedy has been sent to Covent Garden rather than Drury Lane, whisper to Sneer something inaudible to the audience about the Drury Lane manager. 'Writes himself,' agrees Sneer, 'I know he does.'

There is much excellent fun too, at the expense of tired old dramatic conventions, authors' stale set-pieces, actors' clichés. Here, for instance, on the subject of the obligatory 'parting look' before making an exit:

> *Whiskerandos*: One last embrace –
> *Tilburina*: Now – farewell for ever.
> *Whiskerandos*: For ever!
> *Tilburina*: Aye, for ever. (Going.)
> *Puff*: 'Sdeath and fury! – Gadslife! Sir! Madam! if you go out

without a parting look, you might as well dance out – Here, here!

Or of the device, resorted to in one plot after another, of the mistaken relationship, the beggar-maid-no-beggar maid-but-a-mislaid-princess, the orphan-boy-no-orphan-boy-but-heir-to-a-fortune, etc. Here Sheridan was mocking quite explicitly a passage in Richard Cumberland's *The West Indian*:

Justice: No orphan, nor without a friend art thou – I am thy father, *here's* thy mother, *there* thy uncle – this thy first cousin, and those are all your near relations!
Mother: O ecstasy of bliss!
Son: O most unlook'd for happiness!
Justice: O wonderful event! (They faint alternately in one another's arms.)
Puff: There you see relationship, like murder, will out.

Or in a passage like the following, in which supporting characters, turning chorus, contrive not only to think but to speak in unison:

Earl of Leicester: There spoke old England's genius! Then, are we all resolv'd?
All: We are – all resolv'd.
Leicester: To conquer – or be free?
All: To conquer, or be free.
All: All.
Dangle: *Nem. con.*, egad!
Puff: O yes, where they *do* agree on the stage, their unanimity is wonderful!

This *Tragedy Rehearsed* of Mr Puff, by much the major part of *The Critic*, was an essentially topical piece. The danger to the nation after midsummer 1779, when Spain joined France in the war against Britain, was even more alarming than in the preceding year. The threat of invasion, though by the time of *The Critic*'s first performance it had somewhat abated, was acuter than at any time since the days of the Spanish Armada. While the British fleet remained inactive, the enemy for a time had made free of the English Channel. Hence the tragedy's title, *The Spanish Armada*. Hence its burlesque Elizabethan characters, including Tilburina, recalling Elizabeth's rallying call at Tilbury in 1588. Hence the opportunity for a grand spectacular finale to Mr Puff's mighty masterpiece, an apt challenge for de Loutherbourg's impressive artistry and technology, and first-class box-office.

The Critic had its own critics ready to point out some obvious resemblances between Mr Puff's *Tragedy Rehearsed* and *The Rehearsal* (1671) by the Duke of Buckingham. Sheridan's character Puff undoubtedly had his prototype in Buckingham's character Bayes, but Sheridan's textual glances back at this well-known earlier play were overt enough to disarm much of the criticism. In any case, one play showing a rehearsal of another was hardly a novelty – nor had it been, probably, when Shakespeare wrote *A Midsummer Night's Dream*. Garrick in 1767 had put on a play bearing the subtitle *The New Rehearsal*. Moreover, only very shortly before *The Critic* was staged, there had been at Sadler's Wells an entertainment also on the subject of Queen Elizabeth at Tilbury. In this, the *pièce de résistance* had also been 'a striking spectacle in which the Navy of England appears riding triumphant upon the stage' – and the producer of this show was in fact that same Thomas King who first played Sheridan's Mr Puff. But the wit and inventiveness of *The Critic* removed from it any serious imputation of plagiarism. Sheridan was always a liberal borrower and adapter of other men's ideas, and often of earlier ideas of his own too. Indeed, parts of *The Critic* are foreshadowed in a youthful sketch called *Ixion*, done in his Bath days. As for Buckingham's *The Rehearsal*, the success of *The Critic* drove it out of the Drury Lane repertory for ever.

Shortly before Sheridan wrote *The Critic*, Garrick died. He had been a good friend to Sheridan's Drury Lane, despite upsets and resentments. Both Thomases, Linley and Sheridan, had managed to offend him, the latter by taking umbrage when Garrick was invited to a rehearsal to advise on the acting of a part he had once played. But Garrick wrote afterwards to Richard Sheridan, 'I love my ease too well to be thought an interloper . . . Let me assure you, upon my honour, that I am in perfect peace with you all.' Thomas Sheridan, however, was seldom in perfect peace with anyone; not often with his son, and never with the great actor whose fame he never ceased to envy. For Drury Lane, Sheridan's father, stage director for more than three years, eventually became altogether too much of a liability. By 1782 he had been replaced by 'Mr Puff', Thomas King. He was bitterly hurt.

Garrick's funeral in March 1779 was a solemnly grand affair, with Sheridan as chief mourner. In Garrick's honour he also composed a 'monody', spoken from the Drury Lane stage by its leading tragedy actress Mrs Yates, 'with dishevelled hair and in a flowing robe of purple satin'. These were the memorial lines which Byron would later claim were the best of their kind. Thomas Moore rated them rather lower, preferring Sheridan, as most still would to-day, in that *Rape of the Lock* manner better suited to his 'dense epigrammatic style' – shown in the very accomplished epilogue he wrote at about this time to a tragedy by Hannah More. The subject is a bluestocking divided between the claims of intellect and household.

What motley cares Corilla's mind perplex,
Whom maids and metaphors conspire to vex!
In studious deshabille behold her sit,
A letter'd gossip and a housewife wit:
At once invoking, though for different views,
Her gods, her cook, her milliner, her muse.
Round her strew'd room a frippery chaos lies,
A chequer'd wreck of notable and wise.
Bills, books, caps, couplets, combs, a varied mass,
Oppress the toilet and obscure the glass;

[67]

Unfinish'd here an epigram is laid,
And there a mantua-maker's bill unpaid.
There new-born plays foretaste the town's applause,
There dormant patterns pine for future gauze.
A moral essay now is all her care,
A satire next, and then a bill of fare . . .

It is not quite, though it is nearly, true that with *The Critic*, written when he was twenty-seven, Sheridan's career as a dramatist ended. There was a pantomime or harlequinade called *Robinson Crusoe* to come early in 1782 (when it is said that on one occasion the author actually played harlequin Friday). Later, during the 1790s, he put together one or two 'entertainments' of a patriotic nature, celebrating such naval victories as the Glorious First of June and the Battle of Cape St Vincent. Finally in 1799 there was *Pizarro*, a melodrama which again beat the patriotic drum and certainly achieved a big popular success – but is barely recognizable as coming from the pen of the man who twenty years earlier had been widely accepted as the first of living British dramatists. In any case *Pizarro* was largely a translation from the German.

Sheridan did not of course sever his connection with the theatre. For another thirty years after *The Critic* he was still master at Drury Lane and remained dependent on it for his livelihood. He would often touch up other men's work, or sometimes write the 'programme' or scenario for another man's play or opera. He also made many adumbrations, scraps of dialogue, fragmentary sketches for situations, characters, ideas which came into his head, stayed briefly, and departed. Fertile and skilful as he was at turning out witty and near-extemporary verse, he would frequently jot down a few lines which had satisfied him and perhaps might even come in useful somewhere some day. Into the nearest drawer it all went, to remain among the chaos of his papers to be sifted through after his death.

If by the late 1770s Sheridan had become the leading playwright of his day, *that* indeed was satisfactory and warming –

nothing certainly to be sneezed at – yet it was not what his ambitions had been primarily directed at. It was simply not in Sheridan to spend all his remarkable energy and talent in achieving professional perfection and artistic triumph. He had first written plays to give him financial independence. Their success and his business acumen had not only made him London's leading impresario but also made him welcome in those select circles towards which his guiding (or was it perhaps malign?) spirit had always beckoned him, the world of the ruling aristocracy.

5

The aspiring politician

I T was the musical fame of his wife that had first offered Sheridan a passport to the drawing-rooms of the aristocracy, as his enemies often chose to remind him. A publication of 1784, for instance, the *Royal Register*, at a time when he had twice already, if briefly, been a junior minister in the government, was still attacking him for (among much else) making 'by his wife's concerts' an 'acquaintance with the fashionable world' and then 'living in a style of elegance and expense that would soon beggar a large fortune'. Four years later, with Sheridan by that time prominent politically, a hostile but in some respects shrewd critic, Charles Dibdin, the dramatist and musician (composer of the immortal *Tom Bowling*), had this to say:

> Mr Sheridan can write in any style, and to any degree of perfection he pleases, but his public writing, like his public speaking is more *catching* than *captivating*; it dazzles, but does not *impress* – it charms but does not *convince*. In short, as that gentleman's aim is popularity, he does everything for the moment, and it is a question, after he has sunk into ease and independence, from his natural indolence of mind, whether he will ever again be known but by a few eminent trifles . . . Mr Sheridan having most probably done with the stage, as an author, it is but fair to examine how far, in that capacity, he has

been an acquisition to the public; and when we consider that he has deprived the world of the best singer, beyond all comparison, that we have ever heard, it is very doubtful whether what he has given be adequate to what he has taken away . . .

Although after her marriage Elizabeth Sheridan did not perform in public, her singing and her beauty still from time to time enchanted private audiences; always and inevitably 'angelic' in voice and in person. William Wilberforce, the philanthropist and anti-slavery crusader, hearing her at Burlington House in 1783, reported that she 'sang old English songs angelically'. Sir Gilbert Elliot was present on a later occasion in April 1787 when she and her sister Mary 'sang like angels': Mrs Sheridan, Elliot wrote, 'is really nearer one's notion of a muse, or an angel, or some such preternatural or semi-divine personage, than anything I have ever seen alive.' For a semi-divine personage she was highly practical too, and did much both for her husband and her father to assist the affairs of Drury Lane. For some time she kept the accounts, a department of the theatre's affairs emphatically unsuitable to its manager's talents. She sometimes auditioned singers, and helped with the arranging and orchestrating of parts for operas. She could be relied on – always having, as Hannah More observed, the talent to 'write prettily' – to supply words to a song that might be wanting them or, as once to an aria by Gluck, where English translation was required. She would sometimes be consulted on the suitability of plays or entertainments submitted for performance, and at least one of them, *Richard Cœur de Lion*, was adapted for the stage, and possibly also translated, by her from the French original. While her husband's energies during the 1780s were to become increasingly absorbed in politics, her father remained busy with his responsibilities as musical director (working first in collaboration, though seldom harmony, with the stage director Thomas Sheridan, and then after his removal, with Thomas King), and Elizabeth often acted as his unofficial chief assistant, providing help all the more necessary as her father

[71]

became shaken both by the decline in his own health and by the multiplying Linley tragedies suffered over these years.*

When in January 1779 Sheridan stage-managed the impressive pageantry of Garrick's funeral, although he was chief mourner he rode in only the eighth coach of the procession (Linley was away back in the twenty-seventh); the first seven coaches naturally had been assigned to members of the aristocracy. Such a fact, if of no particular importance, does however remind us once more of the obeisance to rank, the almost religious respect for hierarchy, which permeated Georgian society. Sheridan, if he had first broken into its selecter circles through the fame of his wife, had proceeded to confirm his position there by the high reputation and subsequent profits which flowed from his theatrical success, by the charm of his personality, the vivacity of his manners, the liveliness of his wit. Yet though the Sheridans might be welcome and amusing guests in the great houses, their position there – or so at least a part of Sheridan for a long time felt – hard-earned and enjoyable and desirable as it was, was not altogether secure. They were there on their merits, but not by that right which only birth could guarantee.

It was everywhere accepted in Georgian England, alike among rich and poor, that (as Burke put it) 'some decent regulated pre-eminence, some preference given to birth, is neither unnatural nor unjust'. A woman of unaristocratic birth might, though often precariously, win a place among the 'best' society by becoming a rich man's wife or mistress; a man might climb there, first by making money – perhaps in industry or overseas commerce, or perhaps by professional triumphs, as with Garrick and Sheridan himself – and then by acquiring a country estate and mansion, a good address in town, a smart villa perhaps in Hampstead or

---

* Thomas Linley junior, composer and violin virtuoso, falling from a boat on a Lincolnshire lake, was drowned in August 1778. The sailor son, Samuel, died of a fever four months later. Maria, a fine singer in oratorio, died aged twenty-one of 'brain fever' in 1784 – and still to come in Linley's lifetime were the harrowing deaths from consumption of his two eldest daughters, Mary (Mrs Tickell) in 1787 and Elizabeth herself in 1792.

Chiswick or Twickenham, and a supply of servants numerous enough to sustain the condition to which it had pleased God to raise him. Sheridan had neglected none of such things, but something further was needed, both to consolidate what he had won, and to provide a base upon which his ambition might newly build. The eighteenth century did not decry politics or despise politicians as the twentieth is inclined to. Sheridan saw the House of Commons as Chesterfield saw it: 'You must make a figure there, if you would make one in the country.' To be manager of Drury Lane and the author of *The School for Scandal* was not enough.

A number of opposition politicians were already among his friends. John Burgoyne was one, soldier and fellow-dramatist, now in largely unmerited disgrace with the government after his forced surrender to the Americans at Saratoga in 1777. Among the younger Whigs of about Sheridan's own age with whom he was now associating were William Windham (eventually to turn Pittite), Richard Fitzpatrick, and Charles Fox. Fitzpatrick, though still not much over thirty, had been in Parliament for the past ten years as member first for Okehampton and then Tavistock, boroughs under the control of his uncle the Duke of Bedford. The King had refused him a place at Court on the grounds that he did not 'choose to fill' the royal household 'with professed gamesters'. Like Burgoyne, Fitzpatrick had campaigned in the American war and partly from his distaste for it had left the Bedford Whigs to support the 'Rockinghams' and in particular his close friend and fellow gamester Fox, opponents of the war. His sister was married to Fox's elder brother Stephen. Fitzpatrick was an accomplished wit, and his skill in light verse may be noticed in his contribution to Sheridan's *The Critic*, for which he wrote the prologue.

Fitzpatrick was also one of the founders in March 1779 of the very short-lived Whig magazine the *Englishman*, for which Sheridan was soon writing a tough denunciation of George III's war minister Lord George Germain, the man saddled with the unrewarding responsibility of defeating the American rebellion.

Like all the Whig and the journalist critics of Germain's mismanagement, Sheridan could not resist raking over old wounds – for, nineteen years earlier, following his alleged shortcomings on the battlefield of Minden, Lord George Germain (then Lord George Sackville) had been court-martialled and disgraced. 'Are we to forget all former passages,' demanded Sheridan's article, 'and grant him the privilege of obliterating private disgrace by superior guilt of ministerial delinquency . . .? If we elevate a degraded and reprobated officer to direct the military enterprise of the country, why not appoint atheists to the mitre, Jews to the exchequer . . .?' There followed a good deal more in this orthodox opposition vein, with further routine thrusts at the (Scottish) Lord Chancellor, Mansfield, to whose smiles even *Scotchmen* did not 'annex an idea of the purest sincerity', and at the First Lord of the Admiralty, Sandwich, satisfaction at whose claims for the recent improvement in the navy was 'damped by a small alloy of incredulity'. Lord North was let off fairly lightly, being attacked on the familiar grounds of his lethargy and more particularly of the 'fickleness' of his American policy – pursuing simultaneously war and conciliation. Was it not rather as Stephano said of Caliban in Shakespeare's *The Tempest?* ' "What, one body and two voices, a most delicate monster!" ' Lesser political fry such as the historian Gibbon, who had just accepted a post from the government, escaped with merely a little sly sarcasm: 'Some gentlemen, as Mr Gibbon, for instance, while in private they indulge their opinion pretty freely, will yet, in their zeal for the public good, even condescend to accept a place in order to give colour to their confidence in the wisdom of the government.'

A more intimate and old-established friend and ally of Sheridan's at this time – he had known him earlier at Bath – was the man of letters and political satirist Richard Tickell. They more than once collaborated in theatrical ventures (*The Camp*, probably, for one), and Tickell would sometimes act as manager's substitute, Sheridan's 'vicegerent', at Drury Lane. Both men scribbled in the Whig cause, Tickell for a time for the *Morning*

Post and then as contributor to the *Rolliad*; this however did not prevent him and his wife Mary, Mrs Sheridan's sister, from enjoying 'grace and favour' residence in official apartments in Hampton Court – official, since Tickell managed, his anti-governmental activities notwithstanding, to hold a commissionership of stamps worth £200 a year. A harum-scarum and devil-may-care character, he joined Sheridan not only in professional enterprises and political postures, but often also in the preposterous practical jokes and crazy escapades that Sheridan liked perpetrating. And there was at least one occasion on which the joke was *against* Tickell – when Sheridan persuaded Charles Fox to ride with him disguised as a highwayman and hold up Tickell's post-chaise on the Putney Road. Mary Tickell was as devoted to her volatile and unpredictable Richard as Elizabeth was to hers, and indeed the two husbands were no less devoted to their beautiful and estimable wives, though by neither man was this ever reckoned to constitute a ban on amatory excursions elsewhere. (When after seven years of marriage Mary Tickell, suddenly a wraith, was to fall victim to tuberculosis, Tickell first swore eternal widowerhood; left his three children to be cared for by Mrs Sheridan; soon, to her anger, married again; and in 1793 committed suicide by throwing himself from a parapet at Hampton Court.)

It was in Tickell's company that Sheridan first met Charles Fox who, an enthusiastic theatregoer and in his early days amateur actor also, had admired Sheridan from a distance ever since seeing *The Rivals* at Covent Garden. Lord John Townshend claimed to have first introduced the two men to one another. By his account, Fox told him 'after breaking up from dinner', that until that day he had always thought James Hare and Townshend's uncle Charles the wittiest men he had ever met,

but that Sheridan surpassed them both infinitely. Sheridan told me the next day that he was quite lost in admiration of Fox and it was a puzzle to him to say which he admired most, his

[75]

Charles James Fox, by K.A. Hickel: Sheridan entered the political
arena as his ally in the struggle against Pitt and King George III.

commanding superiority of talents and universal knowledge, or his playful fancy, artless manners, and benevolence of heart . . .

As so often, Fox's warmth and sparkle and intellectual force had made an immediate conquest. For Sheridan it was a meeting of the greatest significance.

Charles James Fox, by nearly three years his senior, had been born with many of the advantages that Sheridan lacked. A younger son of Henry Fox, first Lord Holland (one of the leading politicians of his day who had greatly enlarged his already considerable wealth during a spectacularly profitable but harshly criticized career as Paymaster General) Charles Fox on his mother's side was directly descended from the Stuart monarchs, through Charles II's mistress Louise de Keroualle, Duchess of Richmond. He had been a remarkably lively and clever child, soon outstanding in his mastery of classical studies, and then by his father's indulgence precociously and liberally educated in the conventional pleasures of the Georgian aristocrat, wine, women and gambling. By thirty he had become an ambitious politician, originally a Tory junior minister in North's administration, but later emphatically Whig; paunchy, saturnine-faced, darkly beetle-browed; a reckless gambler whose losses, astronomical even in those faro-crazy circles, had already once been met (to the tune of over £100,000, with another £100,000 for his elder brother) by his perhaps too affectionate father; at the same time intellectual and *bon viveur*; shortly to be boon companion of the young Prince of Wales and hence even more strongly than before detested by the Prince's father, George III; prime favourite equally among the sportsmen on Newmarket Heath and his fellow Whigs at Brooks's Club in St James's, whose admiration often came close to adoration.

Leaving aside the King's unique detestation, feelings towards Fox did not everywhere carry such unqualified enthusiasm as among the other high-spirited and wealthy young bloods of Brooks's. He always required to have his supremacy uncontested.

[77]

He was, said George Selwyn, who knew him well, 'intoxicated with the all-sufficiency of his parts', and Horace Walpole, while conceding him brilliant and magnetic gifts, thought that he suffered from 'an excess of vanity and presumption beyond what even flattery and intoxication could warrant'. His gift for friendship was eventually to be matched by his talent for making unwise political judgements, with long years in the wilderness of opposition as a result. But when Sheridan first came to know him well during the late 1770s, the outlook for Fox was still promising, and certainly no-one's reputation stood higher in the world of the great Whig houses, or at least among that majority of them who looked for leadership to the Marquis of Rockingham and to Devonshire House. (The two other main Whig groups at this time, the 'Bedfords' and the 'Chathamite' group round Lord Shelburne, kept their distance.) The Duchess of Devonshire, the dashing irrepressible Georgiana, leader of fashion and a gambler no less reckless than Fox, said of him that his conversation flowed 'piff paff' like the strokes of a brilliant player of billiards: 'he seems to have the particular talent of knowing more about what he is saying and with less pains than anybody else.'

Sheridan entered the political arena under the Fox flag at a time of considerable national crisis. Historians to come would see these years around 1780 as marking the point of take-off for the great industrial revolution which would make Britain for a century, at least, the strongest and wealthiest power in the world, but the promise of such a future was much too close under 1780 eyes to come into focus. The politically conscious public of 1780 had no such vision of things to come. They saw problems and events much more alarmingly: the war in America rumbling on miserably and expensively, though not yet altogether without hope; the Irish, or more particularly the Irish Protestant ruling classes, taking their cue from the Americans and pressing strongly, even it seemed possible rebelliously, for freer trade and less dependence on Westminster; a continuing war with France and Spain (though this, unlike the war with the Americans, was not unpopular); confidence in the navy seriously weakened by

public squabbles among the senior admirals, the chief antagonists each being championed by a rival political party, with the
Whigs indignantly hot in support of Admiral Keppel; the
government, headed by an increasingly exhausted and despon-
dent Lord North, adrift it seemed in ever more turbulent seas.
Indeed the real head of His Majesty's Government appeared to
be His Majesty himself, and it was largely upon King George III
that the fire of Fox and of the Rockingham Whigs became
concentrated. It was this in fact which was to give Fox the least
changing of his political themes over the remaining quarter-
century of his life: in the words of Dunning's famous parliamentary motion of April 1780, the influence of the Crown had
increased, was increasing, and ought to be diminished.

Two months before these opposition sentiments were triumphantly, if fruitlessly, approved in the Commons, Sheridan was
making his first significant appearance on the political scene.
This was the brief heyday of the 'petitioning movement', with its
local 'associations' of would-be reformers. The Yorkshire
freeholders had begun it in December 1779 with a petition
denouncing excessive public expenditure and the abuse of
sinecures, pensions, and other such Court favours. Sixteen other
counties quickly followed suit, and Charles Fox threw himself
vehemently behind the movement, first in Wiltshire, and then in
Westminster, where his friend Sheridan became chairman of a
sub-committee charged with drawing up a programme of
demands. At the head of these, the committee placed two which
for the time were remarkably radical: universal suffrage (by
which was understood universal adult male suffrage) and annual
general elections. At the big public meeting on 2 February in
Westminster Hall, Fox took the chair; Alderman Sawbridge
moved and John Wilkes seconded the adoption of the programme
of demands, and the legend of *Fox populi*, Fox the voice of the
people, was born. His speech to an enthusiastic audience of some
3,000 had the incidental result of his being adopted as parliamentary candidate for the (for those days) highly democratic
constituency of Westminster, with its 12,000 enfranchised

freeholders. He had sat previously, first from the age of nineteen for Midhurst (200 'burgage' voters, easily managed), and then for Malmesbury (voters – just the town corporation, thirteen strong).

Without demeaning or debunking Fox and his Whig colleagues, it must always be remembered that for him, as for his allies like Burke or Windham or Fitzpatrick or Sheridan, expressions such as 'the people', 'the public', 'the nation', carried an unspoken but well understood limitation. Despite occasional lip service to the call for universal suffrage, 'the people' for them did not include the mass of the poor and uneducated, still less the mob. 'The middling sort' perhaps, as Wilkes called them, the men of some small substance, the propertied citizenry, but not the landless country labourers, not servants, not in the towns the propertyless poor; certainly not the drunken mobs who in London for instance surfaced so dangerously and destructively that very summer of 1780 in the Gordon riots. (These incidentally served to bolster popular respect for George III, whose allegedly corrupting influence the Whig politicians were busy attacking. In the local but severe crisis of these anti-Catholic disturbances, it appeared that the King's firmness stood in marked contrast to the indecision of his ministers.) When Fox or Burke spoke so eloquently of 'the nation' they were thinking perhaps of one in a dozen of the nation. Fox the democrat always remained essentially Fox the aristocrat, and it may well be wondered just how long or staunchly Sheridan might have held to his sub-committee's demands for universal suffrage. As for annual parliaments, at least he continued to hold that the existing statutory minimum of seven years was much too long. Speaking in May 1783 in support of Pitt's abortive (and Sheridan thought too timid) bill to reform Parliament, he particularly urged a shortening of the time between elections as a necessary measure 'to correct the great vice in the representation of the people – their subserviency to Government in consequence of their long lease'.

For Sheridan the immediate imperative, with a general election pending in September 1780, was to get a parliamentary seat. He reconnoitred Wootton Bassett, but saw little prospect in that quarter. He went hopefully to Honiton, where he persuaded the artist Ozias Humphrey, a resident there who had painted several of the Linley family, to champion his candidature, but as it proved unsuccessfully. His cause was rescued however by much more powerful support afforded by some of his influential friends, the Crewes, the Spencers, and Georgiana Duchess of Devonshire. The Duchess was very soon to be counted among the closer circles of his acquaintance. She recommended him to her mother Lady Spencer, who in turn recommended him to Lord Spencer's agent, and in view of the 'interest' of the Spencers in the constituency of Stafford, that was the seat already three-quarters won. The severe formality of Sheridan's letter of thanks written a week after it *was* won is a reminder again of his awareness of the need to give rank the deference it expected.

I am entirely at a loss to thank your Grace for the honor and service which your Grace's condescending to interest yourself in my election at Stafford has been to me . . . It is no flattery to say that the Duchess of Devonshire's name commands an implicit admiration whenever it is mentioned . . . I have the honor to be with the greatest respect your Grace's most devoted humble servant R.B. Sheridan.

Sheridan needed to spend some days in the business of wooing voters, an obligatory and quite expensive task costing over £1,000, and, with the necessary post-election constituency-nursing, probably nearer £2,000. He managed to raise the money with his usual resourcefulness, one contributor at least being hooked with the bait of a small share in the profits of Drury Lane. But Sheridan's cash was well spent, for on 12 September, after all the free tickets for 'dinner and six quarts of ale' had been dispensed and all the five-guinea sweeteners to the burgesses had been distributed, Richard Brinsley Sheridan Esq, and the Hon Edward Monckton (son of Lord Galway) were duly declared elected members for the constituency of Stafford. Sheridan was to continue as its member for twenty-six years. Towards the end of that time, when staying with the Prince of Wales at Brighton, he told the diarist Thomas Creevey that after dinner on the day of his first election 'he stole away by himself to speculate upon those prospects of distinguishing himself which had been opened up to him' – 'it was the happiest day of his life'. A petition alleging his election to be invalid because of bribery, a not uncommon move by the losing candidate in those days, was unsuccessful. It was hard, claimed Sheridan in a maiden speech strong in virtuous indignation, that a gentleman should be under the imputation of crimes of which he was innocent; the petition was motivated in malice, and the instigators of such groundless accusations, 'a few of the lowest and most unprincipled voters', should be liable to 'exemplary penalties'. The House listened quietly and attentively. However, when shortly afterwards Sheridan asked Woodfall, the very experienced parliamentary reporter, what he thought of his début as speech-maker, the reply was not encouraging. Woodfall thought Sheridan might do better to concentrate on his theatrical pursuits. Sheridan after pondering a moment declared: 'It is in me; and, by God, it shall come out!'

Sheridan was active from the start on the opposition benches. According to Horace Walpole, admittedly a Whig but by no means a partisan of Sheridan and certainly not of Fox, he 'demolished' in February 1781 a government supporter, John Courtenay, in a debate on the allied subjects of public expenditure, the civil list, and the abuse of pensions and sinecures. The following month, in his first major speech, he introduced a motion – which was rejected – advocating improved police arrangements in Westminster, so that in an emergency such as the Gordon riots of the previous June it would not be necessary to resort to the use of troops. Indeed, he argued, the use of the army to disperse tumultuous assemblies should never be permitted without the prior direction of the local magistracy.

Sheridan did not share Fox's strong personal antagonism

King George III with the Queen and six of his children, by Zoffany: Sheridan was profoundly suspicious of the King's influence in politics.

towards the King, but a common factor in much Whig thinking at this time, particularly among the Rockingham Whigs (or, as they would soon become, the Foxites), was profound suspicion of royal motives, an intense fear of 'prerogative' and Crown influence. When they saw George III instrumental in the decision to call out 'his' army against the Gordon rioters their minds flew back to Charles I. The parliamentary opposition during the first half of George III's reign (and in particular Fox, himself ironically with Stuart blood in his veins) was always conscious of the previous century's constitutional history, and ever inclined to see the spectres of arbitrary power and royal tyranny lurking behind the curtains of St James's Palace and Buckingham House.

By 1780, when Sheridan entered Parliament, George III appeared to have won back some of the authority – in his profoundly conservative view the proper constitutional authority – which had somewhat slipped from the hands of his two predecessors. The Rockingham Whigs, and particularly Fox, though Burke and Fitzpatrick and Sheridan and the rest of his connection hardly less so, were committed to halt that process and reverse it if they could. Fox's own animus against the King was more than political – as indeed the King's was against *him* – and it was to grow during the early 1780s until it became violent, contemptuous, and for a time obsessive. It was 'intolerable', he wrote in 1781, 'that it should be in the power of such a blockhead to do such mischief;' and shortly afterwards he was talking of the King to his friends – according to one of them, George Selwyn – 'under the description of Satan'. As it turned out, that sometimes shrewd and always combative 'blockhead' was to outmanoeuvre Fox in 1783–4 and do him a mischief which in the long term proved politically calamitous both for Fox and for his follower Sheridan.

That lay a year or two ahead. For the first eighteen months of Sheridan's parliamentary career Lord North was still Prime Minister; the war with the Americans – and with the French, the Spaniards, and eventually with the Dutch too – was in its dying stages; the situation in Ireland still held dangers, though these had been temporarily lessened by concessions from Westminster favourable to the Irish counterparts of the English Whigs, the non-Catholic aristocratic and commercial classes. Sheridan did not forget that he was an Irishman by birth and at least largely by ancestry; he was already, and would always be, to the fore when the perennial and too-often desperate problems of Ireland came up for discussion. At this time it was his elder brother Charles who was more immediately involved, having been since 1776 a member of that Dublin Parliament which would never rest satisfied until it had won full legislative independence from Westminster. It was to win it very soon, from the short-lived Rockingham-Fox-Shelburne ministry of 1782 in which Sheridan would have his first taste of minor office, but a most hollow victory it proved. The Dublin Parliament certainly became 'independently' Irish, but unfortunately it was to remain exclusively Protestant and unrepentantly corrupt, and it sat under the shadow of a Dublin Castle executive authority still dominated by Westminster. Born moribund in 1782, it was eventually to be bought out under Pitt's Act of Union in 1800.

Until the long-lived but sorely harassed North administration finally expired in March 1782, Sheridan broadly followed the Fox line. Only a few weeks before North resigned he was on his feet in another attack on governmental incompetence in the conduct of the war, with particular and probably undeserved virulence directed against Sandwich – 'a man', declared Sheridan, 'born for the destruction of the British navy.' Of his general reception and progress in Parliament during these early years the memoirist Nathaniel Wraxall wrote as follows:

Though Sheridan manifested, from the first time that he presented himself to public notice as a speaker, the greatest talents for debate, yet he found many impediments, prejudices, and obstacles to surmount . . . His theatrical connexions as manager of Drury Lane exposed him to attacks which a man of less wit, suavity of disposition and ascertained spirit could not have parried . . . In fact he won his way by superior talent, good humour, and argument . . . powerfully seconded by Fox's steady friendship.

There were already occasions on which he somewhat parted company with Fox, though as yet these concerned subjects other than party-political. He argued strongly in May 1781 against 'adventuring in lotteries', whose proliferation he claimed the government was failing to discourage, partly because it would be taking a share of the profits. For someone who was to be found at Brooks's faro table with Fox, Fitzpatrick, and their fellow-gamesters to speak so unequivocally against 'the vice of gambling' may suggest insincerity. However, it was not the tables at Brooks's or the freedom of the rich to be foolish that he was attacking, but rather the spirit of gambling *among the lower orders of society*, and this on the conventional and respectable grounds that it detracted from 'industrious pursuits' and tended 'to introduce every kind of depravity'. Then the following month Fox, the libertarian, introduced a measure aimed at amending the 1753 Marriage Act and enabling young women from their sixteenth and men from their eighteenth birthday to marry without parental or guardian's consent. Sheridan spoke against the motion. Afterwards Fox rose again, to comment that his 'honourable friend had so much ingenuity of mind that he could contrive to give an argument what turn he pleased'. What Sheridan had done, said Fox, was perversely to speak up for domestic tyranny on the ground of wishing to preserve private liberty. In view of Sheridan's own, and more particularly his wife's, history this sounds puzzlingly improbable. What he *had* said went somewhat as follows: Fox's bill would 'do an injury to that liberty of which he had always shown himself the friend', since

> if girls were allowed to marry at sixteen, they would be abridged of that happy freedom of intercourse which modern custom had introduced between the youth of both sexes, and which was, in his opinion, the best nursery of happy marriages.

[86]

Girls of tender years and immature judgment should not be rushed into marriage, as under Fox's bill they might well be; nor should it be possible for 'young men, when mere boys, in a moment of passion, or perhaps . . . of intoxication' to be 'prevailed upon to make an imprudent match'. In Sheridan's view, Lord Hardwicke's Marriage Act of 1753, laying down that parties intending marriage must first either obtain a private licence or publish banns in church, had had the generally beneficent effect of preventing those 'imprudent matches', often of minors, which before had been so scandalously easy to 'solemnize'. Not often perhaps in his deeds and personal habits but often enough in his convictions and intellectual attitudes there is to be found with Sheridan this considered acceptance of sober conservatism and conventional wisdom.

After North's resignation, the King was obliged to form his next government partly, indeed largely, from the Whig groups. For the second time Lord Rockingham became Prime Minister, though happily from the royal point of view the Fox-Rockingham party were slightly outnumbered in the Cabinet by others, including Lord Shelburne, with whom the King's relations were less strained. Most of the junior members of the new government however were 'Rockinghams' and among them was Sheridan. Fox became one of the two new Secretaries of State, from the start at sixes and sevens with the other Secretary, Shelburne. Burke became Paymaster; Fitzpatrick took an Irish post; Keppel, the Whig admiral in the recent bitter controversies, supplanted the allegedly infamous Sandwich; Fox's uncle the Duke of Richmond became Master of the Ordnance; the Duke of Devonshire's uncle Lord John Cavendish Chancellor of the Exchequer; and Sheridan was appointed Under-Secretary to Fox at £3,000 a year – as it happened the first Under-Secretary in British history specifically 'for foreign affairs'.

He approached his new responsibilities with commendable seriousness, at first even proposing to abandon the managership of Drury Lane, since, as he wrote to Lord Surrey,

. . . I have taken a resolution, which I have confidence enough
in myself to know I can keep, to give myself up thoroughly and
diligently to a business and a pursuit which whether I am right
or not is more to my fancy and feelings [than the theatre] . . .

And in another letter, to his brother Charles, he explained how in
future he would be forcing himself into 'business punctuality and
information', sacrificing 'every other object'.

In the event he did not give up Drury Lane, but left Thomas
King in charge there – in charge, yet as King was constantly to
complain, *not* in charge; never given full authority, always subject
to Sheridan's interference. Perhaps things at Drury Lane might
have gone along more smoothly if Sheridan had sold out – but of
course he could not; it was his prime investment, the source of his
bread and butter, and indeed the jam and cream which he had
come to expect along with it. His theatre's history over these
years is one of continual anxiety and frequent crisis – ventures
failing, fears that Covent Garden was pushing it into second
place, performers at loggerheads with the management and more
than once refusing to appear while their pay continued in arrears.
While Sheridan, the proto-Micawber, was never short of new
schemes and confident hopes, the frequent exasperation of his
acting manager King was matched by the chronic worries of his
musical director Linley.

Elizabeth sometimes did her best to cheer her father up. This
was when he was away for a time in Bath:

You will find that theatrical affairs are going very well . . .
There is no doubt but we shall have a better season this year
than we have ever had. Sheridan thinks the pantomime will do
great things . . . I'm sure we shall all be Croesuses very
soon . . . Sheridan is settling all his affairs very comfortably . . . and he has interested himself a great deal about the
theatre . . .

However, a letter from his other daughter, Mary Tickell, could
hardly have allayed his anxieties. She wrote:

. . . I have been peeping into the accounts by way of amusing myself – bad, bad, very bad indeed. If I can get to speak to Sheridan I shall use my influence to persuade him not to be too cruel – but I suppose we shall see little of him . . .

Some insight into the breathless, brink-of-chaos atmosphere at Drury Lane, the hand-to-mouth condition of its finances, and despite it all the sang-froid of its impresario, may be gained from a hurried and casual-sounding letter of Sheridan's own, to the Covent Garden manager Harris, written in the thick of the governmental crisis of July 1782, the very day after Lord Rockingham died. Sheridan's epistolatory tone is often reminiscent of the company commander who reported from the front that the situation was desperate but not serious:

Dear H. I'll get these six two hundred and fiftys exchanged directly for 12 of £150 and more if I can. Garton [Covent Garden treasurer] has also one of 250 and another of £150 besides those he gave me the receipt for. Which will make £2200. In the meantime I have no possible way to pay Pacchierotto [an Italian castrato singer, whose state of mind, from not having been paid, was 'incendiary'], but by Garton's accepting a note for his last payment – which Pacchierotti will take at 2 months – and he wants to leave England tomorrow . . . [more complications here] . . . I have no other possible way of satisfying Pacchierotti, and it will be the devil and all to detain him. I have paid Pozzi [?Rossi, another Italian singer] and another who are going directly to-day . . .

Sheridan's tenure of his Under-Secretaryship was to prove remarkably brief. Shelburne and Fox found it impossible to work together. In the complicated peace treaty for which preliminary negotiations were in hand, Secretary Shelburne was for bargaining American independence against a general peace to include Britain's European enemies. Secretary Fox, and necessarily Under-Secretary Sheridan, stood for unconditional surrender of American independence; but on this issue Fox was to find himself in a minority within the Cabinet. Sheridan's views on these peace preliminaries had a slant all their own. Nothing should be done to give Americans any opportunity to claim that they *owed their independence to France*. Instead, France must be shown up in her true, that is her entirely self-interested, light: 'I would give France an island or two . . . if it would expose her selfishness, sooner than letting her gain the esteem of the Americans.'

It was in the midst of these protracted negotiations that Lord Rockingham died, after only three months in this his second premiership. Fox thereupon made what in that day was a quite unconstitutional claim which sought to deny the King the right to choose his chief minister. In any case the Fox-Rockinghams possessed no parliamentary majority, and naturally the King chose Shelburne, less of a party man, as his next Prime Minister rather than Fox: Shelburne, Chatham's disciple, the serious-minded, well-informed Whig nobleman, personally very unpopular, but an intellectual and patron of intellectuals, as far removed in spirit and temper from Fox and his hard-drinking, hard-living cronies as could be imagined; Shelburne, whom Fox loathed, and under whom he now refused to serve. Deaf to the advice of his friends and allies, he threw in his hand – which even some of his fervent admirers thought both precipitate and too obviously the result of pique. The political unwisdom of his resignation was soon to be underlined by the desperate, and many thought cynical, step he would find himself contemplating to reverse its effects: an alliance, to topple Shelburne, with the old enemy he had so often and recently vilified, Lord North himself. But for the time being, in the close parliamentary season, he was happy to amuse himself winning or losing the odd few thousand on Newmarket Heath or at Brooks's (where he and Fitzpatrick opened their own faro bank) and enjoying the company of a new mistress – none other than Mrs Robinson, once Drury Lane's and the Prince of Wales's Perdita. From her rooms, so he reported, you could see Lansdowne House, and surely he owed it to his public to keep an eye on Lord Shelburne, who lived there?

Sheridan's loyalty to Fox involved necessarily his removal from the government, along with Burke, Cavendish, and most of the Rockingham group. With Fox his friendship remained close. He was a member of Brooks's himself now, and though never quite in the Fox-Fitzpatrick league of sensational wins and losses, he was soon a willing assistant at the faro table, and always now, with his lively sociability and his gift for conversation and fun, a welcome guest at several of the great Whig houses, notably those presided over by Mrs Crewe (Crewe Hall), Mrs Bouverie (Delapré House), the Duchess of Devonshire (Chatsworth and Devonshire House), and Tom Grenville's sister Lady Williams Wynn (Wynnstay, near Ruabon in Wales).

An often-told anecdote of the admittance of Sheridan to the exclusive Brooks's Club has never been fully authenticated, but it has an authentic Sheridanish flavour about it, and is found in the contemporary and generally reliable Wraxall memoirs, so it may deserve repetition. The story is that George Selwyn and the Earl of Bessborough were known to be ready to blackball this not-quite-clubbable upstart. Therefore during the hours just before the proposed election Sheridan arranged for messages to call these two gentlemen away – daughter's sudden illness – house on fire – hence urgent departures from town, no blackball, and the upstart safely admitted to the Whig holy of holies. His history is full of such unverifiable tales, a large proportion of them relating pranks or practical jokes or witticisms. (A complete book of them was published soon after his death, under the title *Sheridaniana*.) Lord Tankerville remembered Sheridan in his early years at Brooks's, and many years afterwards recalled him there, to the poet and literary patron Samuel Rogers, himself one of Sheridan's companions in his latter years:

> Fox (in his earlier days I mean), Sheridan, Fitzpatrick, etc. led *such* a life! Lord Tankerville assured me that he has played cards at Brooks's from ten o'clock at night till near six o'clock the next afternoon, a waiter standing by to tell them 'whose deal it was'.

In the Commons there were some ninety followers of Fox. They watched hopefully as the terms of the general peace treaty, finally agreed at Versailles early in 1783, were examined and criticized, with support for Shelburne dwindling. Ninety might not outvote the ministerial 140; but ninety plus Lord North's 120 would make a comfortable majority. The prospect was sufficiently inviting for the two principals in the prospective bargain, Fox and North, to attempt a retrospective cancellation of earlier speeches of mutual hostility or contempt. Fox now discovered that some hatreds need not last for ever and that Lord North, the minister whose conduct he had so recently declared to be worthy of impeachment, might make a very acceptable colleague.

Was Sheridan one of those who advised against setting up this opportunist coalition? It seems likely, and indeed in a parliamentary speech some ten months later he specifically declared that it was so – though Lord John Townshend long afterwards said that Sheridan was a 'vapouring rogue' to make such a declaration, and that he had been as hungry as Fox to be back in office.

The new ministry was nominally headed by the Duke of Portland, whose function was largely decorative. In fact its chief ministers were the two Secretaries of State, North and Fox. Sheridan's office, again a minor one, was that of Secretary to the Treasury. One of his earliest duties was to introduce a bill (for raising a £12 million loan) which, as he wrote, got 'abused more and more every day'. Whether or not he had paced up and down for hours (as Moore describes him) trying to dissuade Fox from making his accommodation with North, he was at least clear concerning the effect it had had on the public. Perhaps 'the infamous coalition' would not have seemed quite so infamous and unprincipled if Fox, so vocal as the enemy of corruption, had not himself earlier invested so uncompromisingly in political *principles*. 'No talking will make the Coalition a popular measure,' wrote Sheridan; 'we must do something to convince the people that we are not the worse for it.'

Just before bowing to the inevitable and accepting as ministers men who he said wished to make him their slave, the King had seriously contemplated abdication. As he wrote to the Prince of Wales, the Fox-North coalition left him

> but one step to take without destruction of my principles and my honour; the resigning my Crown, my dear son, to you, quitting this my native country for ever and returning to the dominions of my forefathers . . .

Horace Walpole reported that at Brooks's they were offering wagers on the duration of the reign.

George III of course did not abdicate, but very soon he was privately referring to Fox and his friends as 'my *son*'s ministers'. To make bad worse, the Prince had found among the Whig society at Brooks's and Devonshire House not only amusingly reckless friends and delightful drinking companions, but also useful financial champions. He was nearly twenty-one, and his establishment demanded to be settled. The government, led in this by Mr Secretary Fox, coolly proposed that the £50,000 a year suggested by the King should be doubled. George, not on speaking terms with his 'dear son' (he communicated by letter or via the Queen), was not even on writing terms with Fox. It was therefore to the comparatively innocuous Duke of Portland, First Lord of the Treasury, that he sent a reprimand the like of which few British Prime Ministers can have received from their sovereign. It was impossible, wrote the King, 'to find words expressive enough' of his 'utter indignation and astonishment'.

> When the Duke of Portland came into office I had at least hoped he would have thought himself obliged to have my interest and that of the public at heart, and not have neglected both, to gratify the passions of an ill-advised young man . . . If the Prince of Wales's Establishment is to fall on me, it is a weight I am unable to bear; if on the public I cannot in conscience give my acquiescence to what I deem a shameful squandering of public money.

[93]

In this particular quarrel between the King and 'the Prince's ministers' Sheridan was not a principal. His side however was taken, and for the rest of his parliamentary career he would be seen as being of the Prince's party, 'the Prince of Wales's Friends', even for a time as the chief of his intimate advisers, with all that that implied in terms of political opposition. The angry tussle of 1783 the King won; but the Prince's establishment was not the issue over which the Portland-Fox-North ministry fell. That came a few months later, when the King, choosing in his turn to be 'unconstitutional', took a bold initiative against his ministers. Letting it be known that any member of the House of Lords who voted for Mr Fox's India Bill must be regarded as an 'enemy' of the King, he secured its defeat and hence the downfall of the government. It would be another two decades and more before George could bring himself to admit the possibility of employing Fox again, and as long a time before Fox would forgive his 'chief of villains'.

When Sheridan first became a junior minister under Lord Rockingham, he had used such leverage as he possessed to secure his brother Charles's appointment to the post of Irish Secretary of War. Such an exercise of influence was as much accepted practice with the Whig politicians who railed against the abuse of patronage as with those favourites of the establishment against whom they railed. Burke, for instance, that most passionate crusader in the cause of political purity, found nothing odd or culpable in proceeding, directly he became Paymaster, to secure for his son, his brother, and his namesake William Burke comfortable official positions. Now, as Sheridan followed Fox into opposition (as he felt 'on principle') it irked him that his brother should sit tight on his secretaryship in Dublin, and in a letter to him he could not resist letting him know it: 'You are all so void of principle in Ireland', he wrote, 'that you cannot enter into our situation.' At this his brother returned him a very long and soberly reasoned lecture on the differences between English and Irish politics, explaining how, although his partialities tended towards the Whigs *in England*, the only sensible course for an

Irish minister was to serve his Dublin masters, whose authority was in any case subject to Westminster, and whose first need was 'to have the constant support of an English government' of whatever colour. If there was sense in much of this, Sheridan might perhaps be forgiven for noticing that it also suited his brother's personal book very well, while *he*, who had helped to install him in his cosy niche, sat politically now in the cold. Politically, but not at all otherwise. Certainly he had lost his substantial ministerial salary; and Drury Lane, though its capital value was rising over these years, was never far from a short-term financial crisis. But the lifestyle of the Sheridans was not allowed to suffer any check, despite wistful appeals Elizabeth sometimes made for them to draw in their horns – she could be happy, so she told him (or so perhaps she merely dreamed) in a country cottage. They did move house again. It was not however towards the delights of any rural idyll, but to a select address in Bruton Street off Berkeley Square.

Even politically he was better off than many of his old Commons associates. He was not among the slaughtered in the 1784 election when the young Pitt, at twenty-four, supported by the King and Crown influence, won a big majority and left on the field the blood of some 160 of 'Fox's martyrs'. Neither was Fox one of them, triumphantly returned as he was for Westminster again, against the trend, in that celebrated contest when the Duchess of Devonshire and her sister and the Duchess of Portland so publicly and picturesquely plied their allure on his behalf. Sheridan was brought in again for Stafford, in an election for which a document survives detailing the expenses incurred on his account; 248 burgesses paid five guineas each – £1,302, with underneath a note of the annual costs sustained over the period of the ensuing Parliament (1784–90) in nursing the constituency: ale tickets, £40; 'half the members' plate', £25; subscription to the infirmary £5, and to the clergymen's widows, £2; house-rent and taxes, £23; servant's board and wages, £24; coals, etc, £10 . . . etc, etc, amounting in all to nearly £144 a year, or £863 over the six years. Stafford was reckoned at this time to be among the most expensive venal boroughs to maintain. The agent's total reckoning came to £2,165.

Sheridan represented a corrupt borough, but he spoke up again in the new Parliament for 'sober and temperate' parliamentary reform. This was a subject on which he sided with Pitt on the opposite side of the House (Pitt, still at this stage the vigorous reformer, to his sovereign's pain), and against Burke, his party colleague. To Burke, reform exclusively meant governmental reform – first and foremost the limiting of Crown patronage. *Parliament* was not to be tampered with. Indeed this topic was liable to excite Burke quite immoderately, even to provoke in him 'a scream of passion' against Pitt. It had done so on an earlier Commons occasion in May 1782, when Boswell told Johnson that their esteemed friend had behaved like a madman; and Debrett, the parliamentary reporter, recorded that it was Sheridan who intervened to 'pull down' Burke 'lest his heat should betray him into some intemperate expressions which might offend the House'.

During the 1783/4, 1784/5 and 1785/6 sessions Sheridan's Commons stature quietly grew. 'Of Mr Fox's adherents,' wrote Lord Brougham in retrospect, '. . . the most remarkable certainly was Mr Sheridan, and with all his faults and all his failings

The Right Hon. R. B. SHERIDAN,

Presents the Bearer with

Five Shillings and Sixpence

IN ALE.

Facsimile of an ale ticket issued by Sheridan to voters at an election.

and all his defects, the first in genius and the greatest in power.'
More than just an able quick-witted debater, he proved also a
serious-minded politician ready to treat problems on their merits
and, for the most part, to rise above merely factious opposition.
But this does not mean that when attacked or needled he was not
ready to return the affront with interest. Probably the best
remembered of such exchanges had occurred early in 1783 in an
all-night debate on the proposed terms of peace with France,
Spain, and the Americans. It was never prudent to touch
Sheridan on the one subject above all upon which he remained
most sensitive, his stage origins; and it was Pitt, still then a 'boy'
of twenty-three, who unwisely trespassed. The parliamentary
record recounts:

Mr Pitt . . . was pointedly severe . . . particularly on Mr
Sheridan. No man admired more than he did the abilities of
that right honourable gentleman, the elegant sallies of his
thought, the gay effusions of his fancy, his dramatic turns, and
his epigrammatic points; and if they were reserved for the
proper stage, they would, no doubt, receive . . . the plaudits of
the audience . . . But this was not the proper scene for the
exhibition of these elegancies . . .

Mr Sheridan then rose to an explanation; which having
made, he took notice of that particular sort of personality
which the right honourable gentleman had thought proper to
introduce. He need not comment on it – the propriety, the
taste, the gentlemanly point of it, must have been obvious to
the house. But, said Mr Sheridan, let me assure the right
honourable gentleman that I do now, and will at any time when
he chooses to repeat this sort of allusion, meet it with the most
sincere good humour. Nay, I will say more: flattered and
encouraged by the right honourable gentleman's panegyric on
my talents, if ever I again engage in the compositions he
alludes to, I may be tempted to an act of presumption, to
attempt an improvement on one of Ben Jonson's best
characters, the character of the *Angry Boy* in *The Alchymist*.

[97]

As an extempore counter-put-down, this could not easily be bettered, and Pitt's brother-in-law Stanhope reckoned it 'the severest retort' Pitt 'ever in his life received'. Sheridan was obviously amused by the possibilities inherent in the Ben Jonson reference, for among the huge confusion of the papers he left behind him eventually – unpaid bills, scenes from unfinished plays, scraps of verse, jottings, memoranda, letters as likely as not unanswered – there was found dating from this time a fancifully elaborated *dramatis personae* for his recast *Alchemist*, with Pitt as the Angry Boy, Shelburne as Subtle, the King as Surly, and so on.

The printed account of his part in debates over the next three or four years gives a notion of the scope of his activity on the Foxite benches, though since no verbatim record of his or any other member's actual words was allowed to be printed at that time, the flavour is often missing even when the content is fully suggested. There are speeches on licensing the shooting of game; on smuggling; on the army estimates and the fortification of dockyards; on the civil list; on taxation – of coal, of cotton-stuffs, of female servants; on the problems of governing in India – several of these, introductory to his famous Commons *pièce de résistance* on Warren Hastings which was to come in 1787; and several again on the Irish situation, in particular the terms on which freer trade should be permitted between Ireland and England. Sheridan claimed that certain of Pitt's as it proved abortive proposals could only result in limiting the newly won liberties of the Dublin Parliament; and it was particularly on this Irish question that he became in the mid-1780s the leading opposition spokesman. From Crewe Hall, where she was then a guest, Elizabeth wrote to her friend Mrs Stratford Canning, widow of an Irish banker and aunt by marriage of the future statesman: 'They tell me Sheridan has made the best speech on the Irish business that ever was heard – I hear nothing but his praises.' And in what she conceded was 'an effusion of vanity' to her sister-in-law Lissy, she considered it no partial wife's flattery to say that in the Commons he stood 'second to none but Charles

William Pitt the younger, Prime Minister at the age of twenty-four;
drawn by Isaac Cruikshank.

Fox, in the opinion of all parties'.

'Dick is a very warm friend to the Irish,' wrote Sheridan's sister Betsy to the now-married sister Lissy; 'Mrs S. cannot conceive the violent attachment he has to that country, but from her I found he acts on this occasion from his own feelings, totally independent of any wish his party may have to harass the Minister.'

6

Family tensions

As yet unmarried, Betsy, tied to her father and attendant upon him, was back in England with him again now, for the first of two long stays. She was seeing Elizabeth very frequently and Sheridan himself more occasionally. After their first reunion in September 1784 – it was at the Linleys' in Norfolk Street – she wrote:

> Dick sat by me and ask'd a thousand questions about Ireland that made me smile as one would have supposed I had come from the farthest part of America . . . Dick . . . often renew'd the subject of my Father. He [Dick] is I think greatly alter'd, he is altogether a much larger man than I had form'd an idea of – has a good deal of scurvy in his face, in his manner very kind but rather graver than I expected, indeed I should say rather melancholy than grave. He complains of [his brother] Charles's neglect a good deal as he wished much for some correspondent in Ireland who would have written to him at large on the state of that country.

We may only guess how much of Charles Sheridan went into his brother's creation of Joseph Surface, the man of sentiment and bogus sensibility, the smooth deceiver, in *The School for Scandal*; but it is clear that Betsy Sheridan had no doubts about making the identification. She held her older brother guilty of meanness, and specifically of breaking a promise made to herself and to their father, that he would either help them to open a school in Dublin or, failing that, give them 'a hundred a year each, out of his large income'. Now (May 1785) a letter came from him, 'very sentimental, very Surface-ish', pressing Mr Sheridan senior 'to come over to a little farm he had purchas'd with his *wife's fortunes*' and dwelling much 'on the delight he should have in seeing him by his *fireside*'. Upon this Betsy observed bitterly: 'I confess there is scarce any emetick more powerful to my stomach than an affectation of sensibility.' Thomas Sheridan too was bitter about him ('for my pure gold he return'd me base and worthless metal') – as bitter as he continued to be about the younger son who had refused to let him direct at Drury Lane.

Betsy had been trying hard to promote peace between Sheridan and his father. Once in 1784 she schemed for a reconciliation by arranging a meeting between Thomas Sheridan and his daughter-in-law Elizabeth, but that had merely made him angry with Betsy too; she should have shown solidarity with his rightful resentment. In Sheridan, consideration of his father's crotchety hostility always brought out that vein of 'gravity, or rather melancholy' which his sister was quick to notice. But – no doubt reasonably – nothing would persuade him to contemplate the return of his querulous and quarrelsome parent to authority at Drury Lane. He trod on too many people's corns there – King, Linley, the actors and actresses, everybody. Soon Thomas Sheridan would be off yet again to Ireland, still grumbling, still cosseted by his devotedly loving but long-suffering Betsy.

Denied the position of director, he was still able to claim that he had given Drury Lane at least one pearl beyond price. He it was who had been instrumental in bringing back there, from Bath, after a long lapse, John Kemble's sister, Mrs Siddons – Sarah Siddons of the flashing eye and eloquent gesture, whose histrionic powers mightily impressed even the King, who was not fond of tragedy; the greatest of the tragedy queens; undeniably, from Sheridan's viewpoint, a wonderful box-office draw, and hence one whom it was wise to pay promptly and regularly, when this proved practicable (which was not quite always): Sarah Siddons, the grand lady off stage as well as on, formidably correct and even prudish, with whom, so Sheridan once observed, he would as soon make love as with the Archbishop of Canterbury. Following his sister, John Kemble shortly afterwards joined the Drury Lane company, soon becoming its leading player in tragedy – Coriolanus, Othello to his sister's Desdemona, King John to her Constance, Macbeth to her Lady Macbeth. This last was a part whose sleepwalking scene, by Mrs Siddons's own account, Sheridan tried to insist that she must play *exactly* according to the tradition established by the excellent Mrs Pritchard. As Mrs Siddons protested, apparently carrying the day, how could she possibly do the hand-wringing and out-damned-spotting if Mr Sheridan required her at the same time to *carry the candle?* By 1788 Kemble had succeeded Thomas King as stage director, and although he withdrew later because of 'the eccentricities of Mr Sheridan', he briefly returned before finally transferring to Covent Garden in 1803.

The two leading comedy actresses, and prime public favourites, during the 1780s were Dorothy Jordan and Elizabeth Farren. Among Mrs Jordan's best roles were Lady Teazle, Rosalind in *As You like It* and Imogen in *Cymbeline*; she was famous too for her 'breeches parts', and has remained more famous still, probably, for later becoming the mistress of the Duke of Clarence (William IV to be), by whom in the course of time she would bear ten little Fitzclarences, to bring her full tally of natural offspring to thirteen: a remarkable and amiable woman and a sparkling actress. In their youth Lamb, Hazlitt, and Leigh Hunt all saw her and were all entranced.

Miss Farren was Drury Lane's natural successor to Mrs Abington, whom in fact she followed as Lady Teazle. There survives a note sent by her to Sheridan at his home, which is indicative of the state of affairs backstage at Drury Lane in the 1780s:

Sarah Siddons as Lady Macbeth, with her brother John Kemble as
Macbeth, in the dagger scene from Shakespeare's play performed at
Drury Lane. Painting by Thomas Beach.

Miss Farren compts to Mr Sheridan and informs him she cannot think of playing tonight till he has given an order for their returning the money she has had so unjustly stopt from her this day for not attending rehearsals. She comes out tonight at the danger of her life, has been extremely ill the whole week, and inclined as she always is to do her best to save the managers she cannot but look on their behaviour as the greatest [?. . . illegible] of cruelty and *contempt* she ever knew.

Sheridan, according to his wife, habitually failed to open letters addressed to him, but would stuff them in his pocket and forget them. This however being one of those that he did open, he saw the need to get immediate instructions to Peake, the theatre's treasurer, for the money to be paid and the indispensable Miss Farren to be mollified. Accordingly he set off downstairs, which involved getting past a number of waiting creditors. One Fozard, the keeper of a livery stable, managed to bar his way insisting on payment. Sheridan took him back upstairs, went through a pile of previously unopened letters with him, and 'sure enough £350 were discovered in instalments'. 'Lucky, lucky dog!' said Sheridan, handing over the whole amount, which exceeded the sum due. 'Lucky dog, Fozard; you've hit it this time'.

'He may probably fall into a bustling life,' Sheridan's mother had said. He would need to learn how 'to shift for himself'. Now, in his thirties, 'bustle' was indeed the word. Everywhere he carried with him a sense of busyness and hurry, a determination to miss nothing that was going, to cut a dash, to make a show. His wife did her best to keep up with him; admired his growing parliamentary reputation and his social success; revolved with him as energetically as she was able in that 'whirl of the world' which she sometimes delighted in but now frequently felt was more of a whirl*pool* that was dragging her down and drowning true happiness. 'The life she leads would kill a horse,' wrote her sister-in-law Betsy, 'but she says she must do as other people do;' and this meant parties, and social visits, and cribbage and whist and faro, where she always seemed to lose, and (said her sister Mary) 'going to bed at three and breakfasting at two', and the whole merry-go-round of the fashionable and wealthy.

'Oh my own,' she once wrote to her husband from Crewe Hall where she was parted from him on a visit, "ee can't think how they beat me every night . . . It is the abominable whist they make me play – 21 guineas last night and 15 before . . . I tell you this that you may provide accordingly, for I very much fear you will find no little hoard when you come. But, my soul, when *do* you come?' Later, falling into the loving baby-talk then widely affected in letters between intimates (somewhat like Swift's 'little language'): 'Me want to see 'ee eyes very bad.' And again: 'If you are tired of hearing the same things repeated over and over again, you must bid me not write any more, for I have nothing else to say but that I love 'ee dearer than my life and am very impatient for your return . . . God bless and preserve my dearest love.'

Though their mutual love did remain strong, a degree of suspicion – nothing really serious yet – was present too. Elizabeth was still a notably beautiful woman, and her husband was not immune from nervousness when he heard reports of some man – was it perhaps Mr Fawkener? – paying excessive attention to her. But he must not fret himself, Elizabeth wrote to him; and she was 'vexed' that he should, 'without any shadow of a cause'. It was undoubtedly she who had the more substantial reasons for anxiety. Sheridan's philandering was ingrained and widely commented upon, though it is very likely that several of the conquests he made were as much social as sexual. Sir Gilbert Elliot told Lady Elliot (some years later, in 1789, when Sheridan's extra-marital activities had become notorious) of his 'many fashionable amours';

Sheridan is a great gallant and intriguer among fine ladies. He appears to me a strange choice, having a red face and as ill a look as I ever saw. But he employs . . . not the proper passion in these affairs, but vanity; and he deals in the most intricate plotting and under-plotting, like a Spanish play.

At first it was Mrs Crewe who most troubled Elizabeth, though she long continued with visits to Crewe Hall. Mary Tickell tried to convince her that Mrs Crewe's charms were not quite what they had been in 1777 when as 'Amoret' she was the 'inspirer and model' for *The School for Scandal*, and that Sheridan and she ('the veteran Amoret', as Mary Tickell reassuringly now described her) meant 'nothing but pure innocence'. But Elizabeth could not be sure. From Delapré Abbey, where she was the guest of another Whig hostess and beauty, Mrs Bouverie, whose morals happily were generally reckoned to be proof against siege, Elizabeth wrote sarcastically to her close friend Mrs Canning: 'S— is in town, and so is Mrs Crewe: *I* am in the country, and so is *Mr Crewe*; a very convenient arrangement is it not?'

But by 1786 coolness had developed between Sheridan and Mrs Crewe: 'I believe', he wrote to the Duchess of Devonshire, 'she feels that my heart is set against her, and behaves accordingly.' And two years later Betsy Sheridan (observing incidentally that Mrs Crewe was 'cold' to Mrs Sheridan and was jealous of her friendship with Mrs Bouverie) noted that while Mrs Crewe had earlier had Sheridan 'among other lovers' in her train, now 'as his fame and consequence in life have increas'd, her charms have diminish'd; and, passion no longer the tie between them, his affection, esteem, and attention have return'd to their proper channel . . . He has never seem'd, or I believe, never was in truth, so much attach'd to his wife as of late.' This may not have been untrue, but it certainly was over-optimistic. Sheridan had affairs and philanderings in store, and by then (1788) Elizabeth had only four years to live.

At the same time, the financial troubles of her chronically over-committed husband bore upon Elizabeth at least as heavily as his extra-marital scrapes. There was always the chance of having duns at their elegant door – even the Prince of Wales ran the same risk, rank providing no escape. And there is a story, wholly credible, of Sheridan paying a lightning visit to the pawnbroker's to rescue his silver in order to furnish his table for important guests imminently expected. Away again on a country visit, with Sheridan in town, Elizabeth writes:

> You will never persuade people you are very rich, if you were to spend twice as much as you do, and the world in general, so far from condemning you for restraining, would applaud you for it. Do think of this my dearest Dick and let me have a little quiet *home* that I can enjoy with comfort . . . If you could but get a friend to relieve you from these ruinous annuities at legal interest, it would make us quite happy.

She then scolds him for not telling her about the things she is likely to be interested in, including how her father and mother are, but adds:

> You are a dear good boy my Dick to think of me so regularly when you have so much to do; but if you knew how happy it makes me to get a fiff [note] from you every day you would not grudge the trouble.

There were miscarriages, and only one child of the Sheridans' marriage survived, the boy Tom born in 1775. Intending at first that his son should go to Harrow, Sheridan in 1781 took a long lease of 'a pretty place' near to the school. But Tom never went to Harrow. Instead, after some years at a small private school he was sent away to Hatton in Warwickshire, to board and be tutored, one of a small class of four, by that same Dr Parr who as a young master had once taught Sheridan at Harrow. Elizabeth wept at his departure, but the double dose of sterling common sense needed by any wife of a man such as Sheridan shines out in her correspondence with Dr Parr. Tom had written to her, asking for money, but, she wrote to Parr:

This I have refused, as I do not like to encourage such secret negotiations . . . Will you therefore, my dear Sir, be so obliging as to let him have any allowance you may judge proper for him, and encourage him to make you his friend and confidant on such occasions? Too much money is very bad indeed for children, but a little I think quite necessary, to prevent their being betray'd into little pilfering meanness's, and I daresay you agree with me.

Tom was a lively boy, and Sheridan and he were always to remain devoted to one another. In many ways, some fortunate, some not, he turned out to be a chip off the old block, and every whit as likely to run into scrapes.

Though Tom was now to be away for much of the year, Elizabeth's family responsibilities were soon to be tragically enlarged. Her sister Mary Tickell, well enough to sing with her at a private concert in April 1787, was by May desperately ill from pulmonary tuberculosis. For the next month or two Elizabeth never left her, taking her at last from Hampton Court to Bristol Hot Wells, though she knew from the doctors that Mary's case was hopeless. 'The dear creature', she wrote to Mrs Canning, 'does not seem apprehensive herself of her danger and at times . . . lays schemes for the future that rend my heart.' Mary Tickell died on 27 July 1787, and was buried in Wells Cathedral. Thereafter Elizabeth became mother to her sister's three children, a girl of six and boys of five and three, whom she loved for themselves, she said, but *idolized* because they were Mary's, the children of 'the first and nearest friend of my heart'. It was after her sister's illness and death, and perhaps in part from the strain and grief attaching to them, that Elizabeth's own health, menaced by the same disease, began to worsen. More than ever she longed to be 'out of this noisy, dissipated town'. That might still mean at Crewe Hall; it was from there that Sheridan wrote to Burke in February 1788 explaining that his wife's poor health meant that their return to town, and hence his to the Warren

Hastings business, must be delayed. But from the summer of that year 'out of town' was more likely to mean Dibden (modern Deepdene) near Dorking in Surrey, where the Whig Duke of Norfolk lent Sheridan one of his houses. The surrounding country was beautiful, said Elizabeth, if the house itself less so – but it was big enough to hold Solomon and all his wives.

Warren Hastings

THE career of Sheridan the first, dramatist, the Sheridan whom posterity would most value, reached its peak with *The School for Scandal* and *The Critic* when he was in his mid-twenties. Sheridan the second, the politician and orator, the Sheridan of his own choosing, of his own ambition, was to touch a not much less premature zenith when he was still only in his mid-thirties. The setting of this second burst of brilliant success was Westminster, but its context was improbably exotic – alleged corruption, injustice, and brutality in 'Indostan'; the condoning of judicial murder, the reported violations of the sanctuary and torturing of the eunuchs of the princess's quarters in the palace of Fyzabad, in the Indian state of Oudh. All this was subject matter far removed from Mrs Malaprop or Lady Teazle, from Bath's amatory intrigues or fashionable London's scandalmongers, but it did offer the second Sheridan an irresistible opportunity to bring off his most exciting theatrical sensation of all.

For the 173 years before 1773 the affairs of those areas of India under British control rested entirely upon the authority of the East India Company, a trading concern operating under royal charter. After the decisive victories of the 1750s and 1760s, however, and the consequent wide extension of British influence,

[111]

it was coming to be agreed by politicians that the territories and populations now dominated, and the governmental and military powers now exercised, by the East India Company were much too great to remain altogether outside the province of the Westminster government. In any case the Company, being well represented in Parliament, was itself a political force to be reckoned with. Its popularity in London, however, was low, for although vast profits were obviously accruing to its servants in India, enabling the luckier or more unscrupulous of them – the 'nabobs' – to return to England laden with riches, the Company's corporate affairs were in a condition so distressed that it was obliged to apply to the State for rescue. It was in 1773, seven years before Sheridan entered Parliament, that Lord North's Regulating Act for the first time began to qualify the absolute authority of the East India Company by introducing a small measure of Crown and parliamentary supervision.

It was a time when India, with the empire of the Moghuls in decay, was subject to widespread political disruption and interstate conflict. At first the Company had used puppet Indian governments to defeat its French and Dutch rivals in the competition for trade, but in the process it had become itself, though not in name, an important Indian *government*, willy nilly. By 1765, after the Company's decisive defeat at Buxar of a coalition of Indian princes, the large states of Bengal (with its Nawab now only nominally ruler), of Bihar, and of Orissa all fell completely under Company control. Thenceforth Bengal's substantial tribute was paid no longer to the Moghul emperor in Delhi but to the Company in Calcutta. Oudh's price for remaining, however shakily, independent was to be the payment of an indemnity. In the south, where at Madras the Company was largely autonomous, it gradually absorbed the Carnatic, though in so doing it provoked the powerful hostility of Hyderabad and Mysore. In central India it also confronted the formidable confederacy of the Marathas.

While opportunities at this time multiplied for its employees to enrich themselves by private trading and a variety of

Warren Hastings, president of the East India Company in Bengal, whose trial in Westminster Hall lasted more than seven years. Painting by Joshua Reynolds.

malpractices, the Company's own financial position was being weakened by its expensive wars. Back home, moreover, in the Company's headquarters in Leadenhall Street a complicated struggle was being waged, not too privately, between rival factions mirroring various vendettas between the Company's servants in India. The wealth, presumed to be ill-gotten, of returning 'nabobs' was a frequent object of derision and disdain, and their intrusion into national politics was widely resented. Public opinion was more than ready to believe that for some years past, even decades, the Company's government at Madras and Calcutta had been sullied, at least by unpleasant scandals, possibly by serious crimes. In 1784 even George III was writing to Pitt of 'shocking enormities in India that disgrace human nature'.

A decade before, another Commons committee led by Sheridan's friend Burgoyne had tried unsuccessfully to bring to book the greatest of the nabobs, Clive. On that occasion the Commons, while voting that all the Company's territorial acquisitions ought to belong to the nation, decided to condone Clive's fortune-hunting, since like Othello he had 'done the state some service'. (He had come home with close on a quarter of a million pounds, astonished as he said at his own moderation.) Burke's intended victim now was Clive's successor-but-two, Warren Hastings.

Hastings had been the Company's president in Bengal since 1772, and the following year had become the first Governor General of all the British territories in India. In his thirteen years of troubled authority his achievements were notable. Transferring the government of Bengal from the Nawab's court to Calcutta, he remodelled the administration and subjected it completely to British control. Somehow he managed to organize all the Company's resources, financial and military, to meet the many new threats posed, in particular those from the Marathas in the centre menacing Oudh and the Bombay presidency, and from Haidar Ali of Mysore challenging in the south. These omelettes however were not made without breaking eggs. To maintain revenues adequate for fighting a series of far-from-minor wars he demanded subsidy from subject or client princes, or requisitioned their treasure. Where persuasion failed force was employed, most notoriously against Chait Singh, the Rajah of Benares, and against the dowager princesses (*begums, begams*) of Oudh. His enemies also accused him of securing the judicial murder of Nandakumar ('Nuncomar'), a Bengali official who had accused him of embezzlement.

When Hastings became Governor General he was given a Supreme Council of four advisers who were also intended to act partly as watchdogs. One of the four was Philip Francis who, becoming shocked by the evidence he saw of Company corruption and what he deemed the ruthlessness of the methods employed, fell out with Hastings, fought a duel with him, and returned home full of vengeful bitterness. The evidence he then put before Burke and the Commons committee supplied very combustible fuel for the investigations and helped to send Burke into a white heat of passionate indignation. In 1785 Hastings resigned his office and returned to England, intent on self-vindication.

The following year the Fox party, for whom the East India Company had been a red rag to a bull ever since the defeat of their own Indian proposals in 1783 – the occasion of the King's ejecting them from office – went into action. Their moving spirit and indefatigable organizer was Burke, but Fox, Windham, Grey, Elliot, and Sheridan were in close support. The Company was to be cowed; Hastings was to be punished. Hastings in fact was to be impeached – prosecuted, that is, by the House of Commons in the House of Lords.

It is not necessary to doubt the core of sincerity at Burke's centre, marred though it was by prejudice, error, and vindictiveness. He *was* ashamed of the misdeeds of the Company's moneylenders and profiteers, and disgusted by the alleged brutalities of Hastings' regime. His genuinely was the eloquent voice of an emerging liberal-humanitarian conscience, and the substance of his excited concern is not demolished, even if it must be somewhat diminished, by our awkward knowledge of his own nest-feathering or of the fact, for instance, that his 'ever-dear friend' and namesake William Burke, for whom he managed to secure the handsomely paid Indian paymastership, was as corrupt as any.

Sheridan was not a man to be moved by the same force of moral passion that possessed Burke. Neither, however, is there reason to doubt his sincerity either. He accepted the damning nature of the evidence which Burke had so painstakingly assembled over five years. Though their number was later somewhat reduced, there were at first twenty-two charges listed when Burke initiated his offensive against Hastings before a Committee of the Whole House in February 1786, occupying 103 folio pages of the Commons Journals. Mastering so complicated a brief, attacking on such diverse fronts, would require a team effort, and Burke, though he did not care for Sheridan personally, at this stage still trusted his political soundness, valued his polemical ability, and thought well of his attention to detail, *when he set his mind to it*. He did sometimes have misgivings about Sheridan's reliability, and once wrote to him half-apologizing for seeming over-concerned on this score: 'Do not be surprised that I am somewhat apprehensive of the only fault you have, and which is redeemed by an hundred virtues.' But he need not have worried over the particular matter he was putting into Sheridan's hands. It was soon obvious that Sheridan was taking his Hastings assignment very seriously indeed. 'The Duke of Portland tells me', so Burke wrote to Philip Francis, 'that Sheridan has warmed with a sort of love passion to our Begums.' These were the Oudh dowager princesses whose *zenana* or women's quarters at Fyzabad had allegedly been forced; whose treasure, following Hastings' pressure, had been seized, whose eunuch servants had been put in chains and subjected to 'severities'. Sheridan must have viewed this promising scenario somewhat in the spirit of Lancelot Brown surveying a client's house and grounds: here was capability.

In April 1786 Burke introduced his accusations to the

Commons. In May Hastings came to the House to defend himself. Then in June the opposition, to their own and the general astonishment, secured the vote of the Prime Minister Pitt himself, in support of their motion that Hastings' offences against Chait Singh, Rajah of Benares, gave grounds for impeachment. There followed the usual summer and autumn recess before Parliament reassembled towards the end of January 1787, and a fortnight later Sheridan rose to present the charge in the affair of the Oudh princesses. He spoke for five hours and forty minutes, with magisterial command of detail, great clarity of exposition and expressiveness of voice, and a consummate employment of all the tricks in the orator's trade – rhetoric, humour, irony, sarcasm, an eloquent pathos, a nicely judged appeal to the emotions of sympathy or disgust, a few carefully placed theatrical strokes much in the manner of the elder Pitt twenty-odd years before, and a peroration that could well have gone into one of his own father's books on oratory. Sheridan had begun as a man of the theatre – indeed of course he still was – and he knew the qualities expected of a star performer. The Begums speech marked his triumphant claim to stardom. Even his father, away in Dublin, was at last impressed, and proud of him. Lissy wrote to confirm this 'surprising' piece of information and express her own joy. Brother Charles wrote too, 'as an Irishman', to thank him for the 'high credit' he had done his country.

At Westminster the effect of this speech appears astonishing to us now, unless we grasp to what extent tastes and values, two centuries on, have altered. It was not an age then which had been taught to despise rhetorical effect or oratorical appeal, and to be ever on guard against the emotional blow to the solar plexus. We can hardly believe that although most honourable members contrived to hold back a tear at Sheridan's more poignant passages, some succumbed. As Sir Gilbert Elliot, a future Indian Governor General, confessed to his wife, 'the bone rose repeatedly' in his throat. Pitt admitted that after a speech like that it was almost impossible to vote with a clear mind. Indeed Pitt, whose general hostility to Sheridan is unquestioned, conceded that an abler speech had 'perhaps never been delivered'. His brother the Earl of Chatham wrote that it was 'without any exception one of the most wonderful performances I ever heard'. As the *Gentleman's Magazine* reported, *on all sides* Mr Sheridan's speech was acknowledged 'to be the most astonishing effort of eloquence, argument, and wit'. Wraxall, himself a minor 'nabob' and a government supporter, wrote of it soberly as 'the most splendid display of eloquence and talent which had been exhibited in the House of Commons during the present reign'. And Horace Walpole, a Whig but no friend of Sheridan's, wrote to Lady Ossory, trying hard as ever to be amusedly detached, but admitting the magic of the occasion:

> Mr Sheridan . . . turned everybody's head. One heard everybody in the streets raving on the wonder of that speech; for my part, I cannot believe it was as supernatural as they say – do you believe it was, madam? . . . How should such a fellow as Sheridan, who has no diamonds to bestow, fascinate all the world? Yet witchcraft, no doubt, there has been, for when did simple eloquence ever convince a majority? Mr Pitt and 174 other persons found Mr Hastings guilty last night. Well, at least there is a new crime, *sorcery*, to charge on the opposition.

When Sheridan sat down after his peroration the conventions of the Commons were broken. Traditionally, applause was out of order, but at that moment excitement was such that tradition went by the board. Not only were all his friends 'throwing themselves on his neck in raptures of joy and exultation', but 'the whole House, the members, peers, and strangers, involuntarily joined in a tumult of applause'. Even the 'great shout' which had gone up in Drury Lane when the screen fell to reveal Lady Teazle was nothing to all this. The hour was Sheridan's.

For three further months the opposition pack were snapping and barking at Hastings's heels. Eventually a committee of twenty was appointed to prepare articles, and at last in May 1787 the House passed the motion that Mr Burke 'in the name of the

Commons, do go to the bar of the House of Lords to impeach Warren Hastings'.

Even making every allowance for changed tastes and standards, an attempt today to judge objectively Sheridan's two speeches against Hastings, this of February 1787 in the Commons, and the one to come, of June 1788, in Westminster Hall, would be necessarily futile. They were never written down and nothing approaching an accurate verbatim account was ever printed. The digests supplied in the *Parliamentary History* and contemporary magazines, while adequately conveying the drift, do not begin to suggest the atmosphere, the flavour, the inflections of the voice (musical and resonant, we are told), the command and occasionally the histrionics of the delivery, or of course the extreme thoroughness and precision of the detail. It seems to have been a performance combining the highest skills of the orator, politician, actor, and barrister.

The Westminster Hall speech lay some way ahead, while the processes of the law and the preparation for the solemn occasion ground slowly forward; but the proceedings gave promise of being both spectacular and fashionable. Sheridan's Commons triumph had done wonders for the advance publicity, and tickets were eventually changing hands at prices the Drury Lane manager might well have blinked at – up to fifty guineas each.

Meanwhile there still *was* the management of Drury Lane to be supervised, still troublesome business deals to be negotiated, but still too, happily, a whole world of pleasure to enjoy, of high spirits to expend, of women to be flattered by, of good claret and brandy to drink, of social sunshine to bask in. As for the claret and brandy, already probably rather too much of it. But as he once remarked on being told that so much alcohol would destroy the coat of his stomach – in that case his stomach would have to learn how to digest alcohol in its waistcoat. By now an intimate favourite of the Devonshire House ladies, he was at Chatsworth with them in October, and from there he was due to be off on more country house entertainment, this time with the added diversion of an archery competition. 'Sheridan goes tomorrow,'

Richard Sheridan painted by J. Russell in 1788, the year Warren
Hastings' trial began.

the Duchess wrote to her mother Lady Spencer; 'we kept him today by main force absolutely. He is amazingly entertaining. He is going to Weirstay to shoot for a silver arrow, he is such a boy . . .'

His wife, still grieving for the death of her sister and busy as she was with the three orphaned children, was often, though not always, an absentee from these jaunts and jollities. They were together at Crewe Hall in January, and he and Elizabeth when in town together entertained liberally and expensively in Bruton Street. From about this time two undated letters survive from Elizabeth to the Prince of Wales's private secretary, which show her, now that Sheridan and she were well established in the innermost circles of society, anxious for everything to be *comme il faut*.

I don't know whether I am right in applying to you, but as this is my first attempt at an assembly, if I am sinning against the rules of etiquette, pray excuse it, and in a proper manner inform the Prince that I mean to be at home on the 17th and 24th of this month, and that I hope his Royal Highness will honor me by his company. There will be faro and all sorts of gambling for you . . . If there is anybody about the Prince that I don't know and ought to ask, pray do it for me.

Tuesday
I am going to give you another commission, tho' I know you will soon hate the sight of my handwriting . . . Will you make the proper invitation for me to the Duke of York and his suite? Or tell me how to do it . . .

The trial of Hastings was to begin on 13 February 1788. Only ten days before that, Sheridan was having to apologize to Burke for being 'such a truant from the Committee' which was preparing the prosecution strategy. When he did get back to town, he promised to 'work very hard'; the delay in returning from Crewe Hall, he explained, was because Mrs Sheridan's remaining in the country was 'so necessary for the re-establishing her health'.

Elizabeth had not been well since the strain and trauma of her sister's death the previous summer. But they were both back in London in good time for the trial's opening, calling en route at Dr Parr's to see their boy Tom who, it seems, was 'in great disgrace with his mother', presumably for failing to write to her.

Burke's initial speech for the prosecution in Westminster Hall occupied the first four days – of a trial that was to linger on for more than seven years, before Hastings was finally acquitted. Others of the prosecuting committee followed between February and May. Of the many charges, two had been allocated to Sheridan. The less sensational of these accused Hastings of corruptly accepting gifts. The other was the Sheridan speciality, the iniquities perpetrated against the Begums of Oudh, and it was the promise of a repetition of his admired Begums performance of fifteen months earlier that brought such excited expectancy to Westminster Hall on 3 June, the thirty-second day of the trial.

> The ladies [wrote Gilbert Elliot] are dressed and mobbing it in Palace Yard by six or half after six, and they sit from nine to twelve before business begins. The press was so terrible that I think it possible I may have saved, if not Mrs Morrice's life, at least a limb or two. I could not, however, save her cap, which perished . . .

Queen Charlotte, the Prince of Wales, and the Duke of Orleans were present – in fact all the world and his wife: among them Fanny Burney, feeling sympathy for the luckless Hastings even if he *had* wielded 'tyrant power' (Hannah More was positively a Hastings partisan, indignant against his prosecutors); the ageing Horace Walpole, prepared to savour the occasion's eloquence and drama, adding his customary pinch or two of salt; the historian Edward Gibbon, who rated this second Begums speech 'a display of genius' and was gratified during its second day to hear a reference to his own 'luminous' works ('Did I say "luminous"?' Sheridan asked afterwards with a glint in his eye. 'I meant *vol*uminous'); Gainsborough, who oddly had just made

Sheridan promise to come to his funeral, and catching a chill very possibly in Westminster Hall, sure enough died two months later; Mrs Siddons, who was 'like Niobe, all tears' during Sheridan's highest flights of pathos – some declared that, good actress that she was, she fainted. One who undeniably did faint was Mrs Sheridan. She was present in the company of her friend Mrs Bouverie, and the occasion proved too much for her.

This second great speech of Sheridan's, like Burke's, lasted four days. When at last he concluded, on 13 June, 'My Lords – I have done,' he said, and fell back, perhaps slightly overplaying it, into the supporting arms of Burke. 'What an actor,' commented Gibbon. Calling on him next day, he declared he found him *perfectly* well.

The qualifications in Walpole's assessment seem small against his general praise. He was in an *O tempora, O mores* mood and professed to see England decadent and failing – 'I thought I had outlived my country' – but if it could still produce eloquence of *that* sort, he was 'glad not to leave it desperate'. Elliot considered that Sheridan on this occasion was perhaps not so fine as in the Commons the previous year; all the same, 'it was a very great exertion of talent, understanding, and skill . . . the work of a man of very extraordinary genius.'

Elizabeth was of course elated by her 'dear Dick's triumph' but, as she told Mrs Canning, she was unfortunately 'a little of an invalid again'. She was 'a poor creature who cannot support extremes' – this was to Lissy in Dublin – and still 'suffering from the delightful anxieties' of the previous week. But it was, she claimed proudly, impossible to convey the general delight, astonishment, and adoration. 'Even party prejudice has been overcome . . . What must my feelings be, you can only imagine.'

Unquestionably it all represented brilliant success. But the colours of the picture painted did not hold fast. As soon as the immediate effect of Sheridan's oratory faded, his version of what were very complicated Indian events began to carry less conviction, and may now in parts seem misleading. The *zenana* was never intruded upon. The Begums were mulcted of some treasure, squalidly extracted, but they were only temporarily deprived of their revenues (*jagirs*). One of them did lose a portion of her wealth, to which her title was in any case dubious, but they both remained very far from penury and neither underwent physical hardship. Hastings' defence, especially at the outset, had not been well conducted, and suffered from the knowledge that perhaps his most important witness, the former Resident at Lucknow, Middleton, had become confused and collapsed under Sheridan's examination in the Commons earlier. In general, the record of Warren Hastings in India indeed had blemishes, but the representation of it by Burke, Sheridan, and their associates was largely a travesty.

Two months after completing with such panache the apparent demolition of Warren Hastings, Sheridan was at the bedside of his dying father. Thomas Sheridan, with his daughter Betsy, had recently returned from Ireland a sick man, and later, when Betsy called to tell her brother how matters lay, she was moved to see how moved *he* seemed. 'His eyes filled with tears and his voice choak'd. After embracing me very affectionately he hurried out of the room.' The two peacemakers Betsy and Elizabeth persisting, eventually father and son were brought once more together. 'All pass'd off very well,' Betsy wrote, 'my father a little stately at first but soon thoroughly cordial.' After settling election business, on 10 August the Sheridans, Richard and Elizabeth, set off for Kent, where at Margate Betsy had taken her father for the sea air and sunshine. With them they took the best Westminster physician they knew, to assist or advise the 'medical gentleman' of Margate, a Mr Daniel Jarvis. By this Jarvis's later account, 'the father showed himself to be strongly impressed by his son's attention, saying with emotion, "Oh Dick, I give you a great deal of trouble!"' At 3 a.m. on 12 August Jarvis, watching by the bedside, was relieved by Sheridan, who 'never quitted the house till his father's death' two days later. Amid her grief Betsy declared she found 'a melancholy pleasure' at the goodness of *this* brother's heart (alas, not of Charles's), and 'the truth of his filial affection'.

The public's interest in the trial of Hastings soon faded. So too did Sheridan's, though Burke's persisted obsessively until the tediously long-delayed acquittal. By November – probably before – Sheridan was 'heartily tired' of the affair, so Georgiana Devonshire informed her mother; he wished Hastings 'would run away and Burke after him'. By then very different excitements were pending. The King had gone mad; the Prince expected soon to be Regent; and his followers could hardly contain their pleasurable expectations.

Sheridan, moreover, had for some time neglected Drury Lane. He had bought out Dr Ford's quarter-share in October 1788, but, as usually with him, not by any straightforward cash-down arrangement; and a year later he and Linley between them still seem to have been £9,000 in debt to Ford. At that time Sheridan was trying to give Ford 'an exact statement of our accounts', and explaining rather vaguely and mysteriously, 'The law swallows up our profits and returns us persecution – depend on it I am extracting myself from its grip and shall release you.' But these entanglements at least gave him further reason, or excuse, for backing out of new involvement in the charge against Hastings of corruptly receiving gifts – the 'Presents Charge'. Burke tried approaching him through Elizabeth, but Sheridan was having none of it, and rather lamely sought to assure Burke ('our leader and general') that by withdrawing he would actually be 'helping the cause of impeachment'.

8

The Prince and the regency crisis

DURING the early stages of the Hastings impeachment, Sheridan was prominently involved in two other affairs of much significance for his political standing. The first was the Prince's rumoured marriage to Mrs Fitzherbert. The second was George III's very serious and harrowing first attack of madness, and the so-called regency crisis that resulted. Thus both closely concerned the Prince of Wales.

George Augustus, Prince of Wales and Heir Apparent, 'Prinny', the future Prince Regent (but not nearly soon enough for Sheridan), King George IV-to-be in some thirty years' time, was now a handsome young man of twenty-five – some way yet from Beau Brummell's 'fat friend', but still in the Duchess of Devonshire's judgement 'inclined to be too fat and looks like a woman in men's cloaths'. He had 'a great deal of quickness', she thought, like his father, and certainly did not 'want for understanding'. Emotionally somewhat unstable, aesthetically rather sensitive, a man of moods and passions; recklessly extravagant as he claimed befitted his rank; a 'prince of pleasure' and lover of wine and women; capable of generosity, especially to his many sisters who adored him; generally looked up to by his numerous brothers as the senior member of their generation of 'royals'; mistrusted – or, as he felt, hated – by the King, to whom his heir's dissipated style of life proved so bitter a disappointment

George, Prince of Wales, painted by Thomas Lawrence: his dissipated style of life caused a bitter breach between him and his father, King George III.

that his strong fatherly affection became diverted towards his second son Frederick and some of the younger among his fifteen children.

He was also by now – had been for more than a year – tied to Maria Fitzherbert, a young Roman Catholic widow of good family and some fortune, with whom he fell immoderately in love; who refused to be his mistress; whom he long and passionately importuned; for whom if she continued to deny him he threatened to kill himself, and indeed once stabbed himself to demonstrate the seriousness of his intentions (whereupon she fled for a time abroad); and with whom at last he went through a secret ceremony of marriage according to the Anglican rite. He had in fact called her his wife long before this, and when he made a will twenty years later still used that description. But unfortunately such a union, however sanctified in the eyes of the contracting parties, was undeniably illicit and null under the terms of the statute of 1772 by which the marriage of a member of the royal family required the prior assent of the sovereign. There was also the eighty-five-year-old Act of Settlement by which, if he married a Roman Catholic, the Prince disqualified himself from the succession.

To the Whigs, the possibility that this unpredictable and hardly sex-starved young man might actually be prepared to disinherit himself for love of an insistently virtuous Catholic widow was too shocking to consider. He was 'their' Prince and Heir Apparent, just as George III had once referred to them as 'my son's ministers'. Disinheriting himself, he would disinherit them too. Rumours of the existence of this guarantee for party catastrophe circulated for many months, since not even a very secret marriage, requiring witnesses, was likely to stay quite secret. Even Burke, absorbed as he was with his Warren Hastings preparations, was worried enough to write at length on the subject to Windham. The Prince, he said, must get properly and legally married to some European Protestant princess, and have children; the family of the nation needed a family man as its head and symbol.

That the Prince's attachment to Maria Fitzherbert was more than a mere liaison was positively known by only a very few, and Fox and Sheridan were not among them. Naturally they heard rumours, and Fox at least had discussed the event's possibility before it happened. Hence, ten days before the ceremony took place at Mrs Fitzherbert's house, he wrote to the Prince earnestly advising him against the folly of a 'concealed' or 'mock' marriage, and the Prince's reply had been blandly dismissive:

. . . Make yourself easy, my dear friend; believe me the world will now soon be convinced that there not only is not, but never was, any ground for these reports which of late have so malevolently been circulated.

In April 1787 the Commons were debating the evergreen topics of the Prince of Wales's financial establishment and his debts, more grossly swollen than ever now that he was building Carlton House. Fox, Sheridan, and their friends were pressing for a prompt and generous settlement, and the King, though not unprepared for it, was wanting to see, as preliminary, some earnest of filial good sense and good housekeeping – though hardly perhaps of good will, of which he might reasonably have been unhopeful. Then, in the middle of this debate, a pro-government backbencher, John Rolle, was bold enough (in code language universally understood) to raise the matter of the rumoured marriage. Fox, trusting the Prince's earlier denial, and moreover clearly implying that he had the Prince's authority for what he now said, flatly repudiated the suggestion that there had been any such ceremony.

Mrs Fitzherbert exploded in tearful outrage; it was said that she never spoke to Fox again. The Prince floundered miserably in the hole he had dug for himself, trying to convince himself that he would have the resolution to go through with what he had for some time been threatening – to renounce his right to the succession and live abroad with his adored Maria. Of course, he did neither. He settled for Carlton House and Brighton instead.

Fox and the Prince of Wales were never cronies again, and for a year or so were hardly on speaking terms. Meanwhile someone had to be found to say something in the Commons, if not to put things right – that was impossible – at least to make the best of so very bad a job. Who but Sheridan? On 4 May 1787, therefore – it was a month before his Westminster Hall oration – it was he who was called upon to steer between the Scylla of admitting this marriage-nonmarriage and the Charybdis of further distressing the Prince or his already profoundly wounded partner. With some dexterity Sheridan contrived to navigate these perilous waters, discreetly enveloped in a fog of judicious verbiage. *Of course* 'no attempt had at any time been made to screen' from parliamentary view any part of the Prince's 'conduct, actions, or situation'; and Parliament itself, by not pressing the Prince too hard, had done credit to its own 'decorum, feelings, and dignity':

> But . . . he must take the liberty of saying . . . that there was another person entitled, in every delicate and honourable mind, to the same attention [as His Royal Highness] – one whom he would not otherwise venture to describe or allude to, but by saying it was a name which malice or ignorance alone could attempt to injure, and whose conduct and character claimed and were entitled to the truest respect.

Mrs Fitzherbert was grateful and somewhat mollified, which did wonders both for the Prince's state of mind and for Sheridan's standing with him. It is from about this time that Sheridan may be regarded as the Prince of Wales's principal parliamentary adviser, even supplanting Fox. And of course, as the months went by, the Prince had increasingly to recognize that the concealed marriage against which Fox had warned him *must* be a nonmarriage; that he would some day be King and perhaps, even very soon, might be Regent; and that he was probably, if only to get himself out of debt, doomed one day to marry some unbearable, very likely ugly, but safely Protestant German princess.

The prospect of an imminent regency arose from a sudden severe deterioration in the King's health in the autumn of 1788. George III, who until he was fifty had in general enjoyed notable vigour of both body and mind, had been unwell in the summer, had then apparently recovered, but in October developed alarming symptoms.

Suffering first from abdominal pain, difficulty in breathing, and nocturnal cramps, he was soon a victim to insomnia, overpowering nervous excitement, and an inability to control a gabbling loquacity. By early November he was hallucinating and often delirious. Bouts of verbal vehemence and physical violence were followed by periods of lassitude and despair. On one or two occasions he lapsed into coma after convulsions, and for a time it was considered probable that he was about to die. At least it became obvious that, with the monarch so wildly deranged, and unless there were some sudden unexpected recovery, there must soon be a regency. Captain Payne, the Prince's comptroller and personal secretary – who had been promised a Lordship of the Admiralty under the expected new dispensation – reported optimistically that the royal pulse was becoming daily weaker. Stories of the King's violent and irrational behaviour grew ever more extravagant and sensational.

Fox was out of the country that autumn, touring in Italy with Mrs Armistead, but in London Sheridan and the other Whig leaders were agog with the expectation of office and eager for the scraps of news – hard news and rumours – that came to them in London via the doctors or the royal pages and other attendants, or sometimes from the Prince of Wales and Duke of York themselves, so long as they were still at Windsor with their father and mother. (The rather over-eager Prince and his distraught mother were soon quarrelling.) In these early days of the King's malady there were seven doctors at Windsor, headed by the Prince of Wales's own Dr Warren, whom the King detested so fiercely that he would not let him get near the bed – the royal pulse was taken by relay with Warren listening at the door. But towards the end of November the King was tricked into allowing himself to be taken to Kew, which he did not like but which was more convenient for physicians and politicians alike, being nearer London. At much the same time a new doctor appeared on the scene, Pitt's man Addington to balance the Prince's man Warren.

The news from London caught up with Fox at Bologna. Hurrying home without Mrs Armistead, he heard a false report at Lyon that the King was already dead. It was not until 24 November that he arrived back, 'tired and grown very thin' as the Duchess of Devonshire noted. Two days later she reported him being in conference with Sheridan, the Prince, and the Duke of York at the Fox country house near Chertsey, and that same day she wrote that the Prince had 'summoned all the Cabinet'. The ministerial chickens were being counted; already they were *the Cabinet*.

The Prince's chief adviser before Fox's return, Sheridan remained so even afterwards, which did not entirely please everyone and naturally not Fox. 'Sheridan keeps his hold with the Prince,' wrote Georgiana Devonshire, First Lady of the Whigs; he was 'deservedly high in the Prince's favour'. And then – 'The Prince praised Sheridan very much, and said he had played his cards well, for he has devoted himself to a man who is not insensible of his merits.' And it was *by Sheridan* that the Prince had just written her 'a kind letter'. 'Sheridan wishes it to be a true Rockingham administration,' she wrote, and it would be one, according to her, in which 'Sheridan might certainly be the Chancellor of the Exchequer if he chuses', though she thought he would 'prefer reaching it by degrees and when he has proved his capability to the public'. Not everybody however welcomed the prospect of Sheridan in charge of the nation's finances, in view of a certain notoriety surrounding those of Drury Lane. And there were still many who thought of him as an upstart. William Eden, the future Lord Malmesbury, observed frostily that the time was hardly ripe for the manager of Drury Lane Theatre to become His Majesty's Chancellor of the Exchequer. In the end it was agreed that he would become Navy Treasurer, at the far from derisory salary of £4,000 a year.

By early December the King was put under the charge of Dr Willis, a 'mad-specialist', who brought with him not only his own tried methods of treatment – which included subjection when necessary to the fearsome strait-waistcoat – but also a new sense of optimism, which he succeeded in passing on to the King's friends and supporters, and not least the Queen. Previously her shock and horror from recent events, and anxiety for their outcome, had been matched by her fury at the Prince's insensitive behaviour; he so obviously could hardly wait to take up the reins of authority. The Whigs were confirmed in their belief that the Queen was a termagant and hostile to them; and the Prince once went so far as to say to her, 'Madam, I believe you are as much deranged as the King.' From the time of the Willises' arrival – there were two of them, father and son – it seemed not merely probable that the King would survive: he might even recover sanity, and that could hardly portend altogether well for the Prince, for Fox, or for Sheridan the 'prentice ministry-maker.

That same December 1788 there began too the long parliamentary debates upon the proposed regency. The Whigs demanded that it should be unrestricted and vested exclusively in the Prince of Wales. Pitt, of course with a parliamentary majority behind him, proposed important limitations to the regent's authority. These, *inter alia*, would have left him without the power to create peers and with severely restricted rights to grant pensions and places – which would have meant that his new ministers would be forced to come to some arrangement with Pitt.

It was at this point that the Whigs' jaunty confidence of the previous month became clouded by internal differences and clashes of personality. Fox did not help matters by being made to seem clumsy in the Commons debates, and Pitt with some justice could claim to have 'unwhigged' his opponent by making it appear that it was Fox who stood strongly in favour of the regent's absolute right, while Pitt and his ministers stood for constitutional parliamentary controls. On this question of 'limitations' Sheridan (at least privately) differed with Fox and certainly thought he had mishandled the debate. Accept the restrictions for the time being, argued Sheridan, and then repeal them when the Whigs come to office. No, said Fox, fight now: 'I always believe in taking the bull by the horns.' Maybe, said Sheridan, 'but you need not have drove him into the room' first. Another matter on which Fox and Sheridan parted company concerned Pitt's Lord Chancellor, Thurlow, who was a personal friend of the King, though disliked by Pitt himself. With the Prince of Wales's backing, Sheridan entered into long and delicate negotiations with Thurlow, hoping to persuade him – the Chancellorship was then an office of prime importance – to adopt a position of party neutrality and continue on the Woolsack with a future Whig government. When Thurlow, noting no doubt the new optimistic Willis atmosphere, at last declared publicly for the existing administration, both Sheridan and the Prince were disappointed, but Fox privately declared himself 'very happy'.

The Duchess of Devonshire's diary gives evidence enough of the internal jealousies and mutual irritations which beset the Whig camp.

> *Saturday 20 December.* Fox was angry with Sheridan yester-day . . . then made him excuses for having snubb'd him – and Sheridan said quite as to a child, pooh pooh be as cross as you will . . .
>
> *2d of Janry.* [Sheridan having failed to perform in time something he had promised] Charles spoke crossly to him . . . to which Sheridan answer'd – I am as God made me and hate personalitys, and they have been boudéing [sulking with] each other all day.
>
> *Friday 9* . . . Sheridan was in a great rage and laid about him of friend and foe . . .
>
> *Sunday 11* . . . Nothing but treachery going forward – Sheridan hears Grey has abus'd him, Grey is abus'd by the others.

The Prince's carefully pondered reply to Pitt, largely surrendering, under protest, to his terms for restricting the regent's powers, was first drafted in various versions by Burke; but these proving unsatisfactory, Sheridan was called on in some haste to compose another, which was done, no doubt in his customary scrawl. The fair copy for dispatch was in the very legible handwriting of his wife. It was rushed to Carlton House before Fox was given a chance to revise it, which did not please him.

But there was to be, after all, no statute of limitations and no regency for another twenty-two years. Pitt would not have to retreat to practise law, which he had been talking about. Fox, intermittently ill ever since returning from Italy, and now recuperating at Bath, had his bitterest pill to swallow. The King began to recover. Fanny Burney, at this time a servant of the Queen, walking in the gardens at Kew, suddenly to her initial panic found herself being vigorously pursued by the King himself, who catching her up seemed *almost* himself again, though still over-excited. He put his hands on her shoulders, kissed her kindly on the cheek, and told her not to worry – he would look after her. The long battle of the rival doctors' medical bulletins (the Prince of Wales's Dr Warren versus the Willises) ended. Soon His Majesty was well advanced in convalescence, though not yet ready to forgive his two eldest sons' recent behaviour. Sheridan would *not* be Navy Treasurer. The Whigs would, as it turned out, be in opposition, first for another seventeen years, and then after a brief interlude for even longer. The bright vision had been a mirage.

While the King had been fighting his long, traumatic, and sometimes grotesque battle against his disease and his doctors; while the Commons had been debating the 'limitations' and Sheridan had been parleying with Lord Thurlow; while day by day Georgiana Devonshire had been jotting down so knowledgeably and revealingly all the Whig comings and goings – all this time across the Channel the ministers of Louis XVI had been preparing for an occasion of supreme moment, the meeting after a lapse of 165 years of the French parliamentary estates, the States General. Its summoning, and the revolution and wars which followed during the next quarter-century – almost exactly the years remaining to Sheridan – would have wide and serious consequence for him, for Fox and Burke (for it sundered them), for Whigs, Tories, and British party politics in general, and indeed for the whole of Europe and a good deal for the rest of the world. The States General met in May 1789, the same month in which Charles Fox was still trying to persuade himself that George III had *not* recovered – 'As to the poor man, he is mad', he was writing to Mrs Armistead – though there had already been at St Paul's a Grand Thanksgiving for that very recovery. The Hastings trial continued in that May and June. Sheridan's sister Betsy went there once or twice and 'felt a thousand pulses beat' as her brother rose to speak; his manner so like their father's; his 'calm dignity'; his voice 'uncommonly fine' and *perfectly* audible, 'which is surprising as you know his general way of speaking is rather slovenly'. There were grand assemblies and balls for Betsy to attend too when she wished, though she tended to shy away from such occasions when she could, and several times noted how bad they were for Elizabeth – 'raking at Bolton House', for instance, till four in the morning and as a result 'quite knocked up'. But Betsy did go to a very splendid masquerade at Hammersmith in June with the Prince present (she was introduced), and the Royal Dukes and half the *beau monde* of London – and Lady Duncannon who, Betsy acidly remarked, cast 'many tender looks towards Dick, which to my great joy did not seem much attended to'. Betsy disapproved hugely of Lady Duncannon (the Duchess of Devonshire's younger sister) as of other siren beauties luring her brother away from that kindest and in every way most estimable woman his wife. Lovely too as ever: 'After we all unmask'd Dick walk'd about a good deal with us and several of the masks remark'd that having such a partner it was no wonder he kept by her: I think I never saw Mrs S— look handsomer.' Sheridan was obviously in characteristic form:

Dick who came in a black domino put on a disguise after supper and made a great deal of diversion, as he was unknown to everyone but us; having plagued several people sufficiently he resumed his domino and return'd to the company, pretending he had just left a party at supper, and at length at a shamefully late or rather early hour we return'd to town.

Unfortunately Betsy was right to be worrying about Lady Duncannon and those tender looks.

9

'She is an angel, it is all my fault'

UNEASINESS between Sheridan and Elizabeth did not arise exclusively from his extra-conjugal adventures. His immoderate drinking also provided occasions of disharmony. 'When you tell me', she wrote, 'how vexed and grieved you was at not being able to speak that Monday, on account of your making yourself so ill on Sunday, would you have me say, drinking to that extent is not an *abominable habit*?' And as often before, after the regency débacle Elizabeth tried to persuade him that he had become too heavily engaged in the exhausting political battle. It kept them so long apart. Betsy Sheridan – just now to become Mrs Henry Lefanu* – observed at this time how her brother was seldom at home two days together. Quite natural and inevitable, Elizabeth replied to Betsy; but to Sheridan she wrote: 'I am more than ever convinced we must look to other resources for wealth and independence, and consider politics as a mere amusement – and in that light 'tis best to be in opposition.' He could not see things that way.

She worried too about his ever-ambitious but never other than contorted theatrical dealings, in crisis again just now over negotiation with the Covent Garden manager, Harris. 'I can't make out', protested Elizabeth, 'what business you are settling

---

* Lissy (Alicia) was Mrs Joseph Lefanu, married to the elder brother.

with Harris . . . I have no opinion of Mr H. nor ever had. He is selfish, quite a man of the world, of course *you* are no match for him; but I trust you do not deceive me when you say you shall settle things *well* . . .' And eloquently she protested again after he had actually complained that her letters seemed to betray a certain 'coldness':

> Might not I as well accuse you of coldness, for not filling your letter with professions, when your head must be full of business? I think of nothing all day long but how to do good, somehow or other, for you . . .

But of course it was Sheridan's incurably roving eye that lay behind much of the trouble that was brewing: what Elizabeth's devotedly kind but strictly moral friend Mrs Canning ('Sister Christian', Elizabeth called her) described as his 'long habits of self-indulgence'.

'Lady Duncannon is, thank God, gone to Bruxelles,' the newly married Betsy wrote to her sister Lissy in March 1790. 'I should not be sorry to hear she was drown'd on her way thither.'

Henrietta Frances (second daughter of Earl Spencer and wife of Lord Duncannon, heir to the earldom of Bessborough) was the latest and socially most exalted of Sheridan's conquests. The busy days of the regency crisis had meant that he had been at Devonshire House, a main Whig headquarters, even more frequently than usual, and so had seen a great deal of the feminine trio at the heart of it: Georgiana, the Duchess, who 'effaced all', as Walpole put it, 'without being a beauty'; Lady Elizabeth Foster, the Duke's current mistress and Georgiana's eventual successor as Duchess; and Henrietta, or Harriet, Duncannon, the youngest of the trio, with whom Sheridan fell in love – far from trivially or casually – and who soon warmly returned his advances. Lady Duncannon was the mother of the little girl, now only five years old, who would grow up to be that headstrong and tempestuous Lady Caroline Lamb, the young Melbourne's wife, whose publicly conducted sexual hostilities with Byron would make her

Georgiana, Duchess of Devonshire, the dazzling leader of Whig society, and her younger sister, Lady Duncannon, with whom Sheridan fell in love. Pen and watercolour by Rowlandson.

mother's earlier adventure with Sheridan seem tame by comparison.

At this time Lady Duncannon's sister, the Duchess Georgiana, was involved in an affair with Sheridan's younger Whig colleague Charles Grey, the future Earl and Prime Minister, whose child she would soon be bearing in 'exile' and secrecy, at Aix-en-Provence – some seven years after Lady Elizabeth Foster had been to France on a similar errand carrying the Duke's daughter. Sexual behaviour at Devonshire House had its own code, obscure to outsiders, sometimes apparently bizarre – but Lady Duncannon was by no means an idle flirt or wanton (indeed she was religiously inclined), and the Duchess, however reckless and in the end self-destructive, was a woman of integrity and intelligence, of warm generosity and infinite charm. (She swore, incidentally, that Grey was her 'one and only' lover.) In Sheridan's letters – nobody has discovered why – she is 'T.L.'; he writes to her as an intimate, though not sexually intimate, friend.

The letters to Lady Duncannon – or rather those parts of them which survive the erasures which she made (presumably it was she) after the fires had cooled – are an odd jumble of political comment and playful allusion, occasionally echoing the modish Devonshire House baby-talk: 'I must bid *oo* good-night for by the light passing to and fro near your room I hope you are going to bed, and to sleep happily, with a hundred little cherubs fanning their white wings over you . . . Now draw the curtain Sally.' (Sally was Lady Duncannon's personal maid.)

Discovery of the existence of the liaison led Lord Duncannon by midsummer 1789 to begin proceedings against Sheridan under the old common-law charge of 'crim. con.' – that is, criminal conversation, adultery regarded as trespass against the wronged husband. This as it happened was just as Elizabeth Sheridan was ill again, and suffering another miscarriage, while her husband was away at Brighton for celebrations of the Duke of York's birthday.

With Sheridan known to be an inveterate womanizer, and his beautiful wife living as she did constantly amid the whirl and dazzle of high society, it is not surprising that plenty of masculine eyes turned hopefully in her beguiling direction. The world in which the Sheridans moved was hardly (to put the matter at its lowest) one strictly observing the commands of monogamy. As early as 1786 Mary Tickell had one day opened by mistake a letter addressed to her sister, read there what was not for a third party's eyes, and been sworn to secrecy. Then Elizabeth herself once mentioned to strict-minded Mrs Canning certain 'peccadilloes' of hers upon which 'now that everything is blown over' she hoped silence would prevail. A visit to the house at East Burnham where her honeymoon had been spent prompted not only a lovingly reminiscent letter to Sheridan and some nostalgic tears, but (again to Mrs Canning) a mysterious though perhaps not in itself incriminating admission that she had 'tasted the forbidden fruit since that time'. Betsy, while always singing her sister-in-law's praises, was also constantly deprecating the rackety life she had taken to leading, and Elizabeth herself in June 1790, with Sheridan away again (this time electioneering in Stafford) wrote to him:

> . . . Now for my journal, sir . . . I was at home all day busy for you, went to the Opera, afterwards to Mrs St John's, where I lost my money sadly, sir . . . sat between Lord Salisbury and Mr Meynell (hope you approve of that, sir) . . . and on [Sunday] evening at Lady Hampden's lost my money again, sir, and came home by one o'clock. I have promised to dine with Mrs Crewe who is to have a female party only, no objection to that I suppose, sir?

Once or twice about this time she felt the need to defend her code of morality both to her sister-in-law and to 'Sister Christian'. She was by no means ashamed that it was not quite so demandingly proper as theirs.

The most persevering of her admirers at this time was none other than the King's third son, the young Prince William, now Duke of Clarence, one day to be King William IV. He took to visiting her at Richmond every morning, and although she rejected his advances she admitted even to the shockable Hitty Canning that she was 'not indifferent to his devoted attachment'. Accepting defeat, the Duke turned instead towards Drury Lane's current queen of comedy (that very year playing Lydia Languish there), the sparkling, accessible, and as it turned out prolific and durable Mrs Jordan, who remained his all-but-wife for the next twenty years.

When the Duncannon affair touched crisis point it was from Crewe Hall that Elizabeth unbosomed herself of the whole distressing story to Mrs Canning. There were 'a thousand causes for vexation' between herself and Sheridan, and they had decided upon 'an amicable separation'.

We have been for some time separated in fact as man and wife. The world, my dear Hitty, is a bad one, and we are both victims of its seductions. Sheridan has involved himself by his gallantries and cannot retreat. The duplicity of his conduct to me has hurt me more than anything else, and I confess to you that my heart is entirely alienated from him.

She would not, she continued, do anything to disgrace either herself or her family, and she would not be becoming the Duke of Clarence's mistress. The last straw at Crewe Hall had been Sheridan's conduct just *after* he had been praying for her forgiveness, 'imprecating all sorts of curses upon himself' and promising reformation.

He threw the whole family at Crewe into confusion and distress by playing the fool with Miss F. (little Emma's governess) and contriving so awkwardly too as to be discovered by the whole house locked up with her in a bed-chamber in an unfrequented part . . . I am confident that if the Duke of Clarence had been six and thirty instead of six and twenty I should have run away with him immediately, and most probably should have hung myself a week afterwards.

But the Sheridans' parting was only brief. The Duke of Devonshire managed to persuade Lord Duncannon to drop legal proceedings, while Lady Duncannon undertook to go abroad for a while. Charles Fox, Mrs Bouverie, and Sheridan himself succeeded in talking Elizabeth back into giving him one more chance. So 'in some sort', as she wrote, matters were made up: 'I have received him once more into favour, though I own to you I have lost all confidence in his professions and promises.'

Very soon after this, a new figure entered Elizabeth's world: Charles Fox's Irish cousin Lord Edward Fitzgerald, brother of the Duke of Leinster, nine years Elizabeth's junior, an army officer, handsome, a romantic idealist. Not many years later he would secure his place in Ireland's tragic history as the passionate revolutionary of 1798, dead in prison after the failed rebellion, ever to be revered in the book of Irish republican martyrs. In 1791, not yet the full convert to Jacobinism that he soon would be, and during his English stay seeing much of Fox and his followers (including of course the Sheridans, at the grandly expensive Isleworth Thames-side mansion they had recently taken), he, like so many before him, fell in love with Elizabeth and by midsummer she was pregnant with his child.

'I have been leading a strangely raffish life recently,' she confessed to Mrs Canning; one day, she promised, she would 'come to a true confession.' Again she was far from well, and was soon leaving Isleworth for Tunbridge Wells, where that 'eccentric being' Sheridan 'without saying a word' to her, but perhaps really for her health's sake, took yet another house. Then by January 1792 she was at Southampton 'for the air'. Here Fitzgerald, stationed then at Portsmouth, would be in a position to visit her. 'During her illness at Southampton and in town,' he wrote to his mother later, 'she must have seen how truly I loved her. Indeed she told [me] she did, and owned it almost made up for her being so ill.'

By now Sheridan, commuting between parliamentary business in town and visits to Southampton, had become seriously worried for her, and his spirits fluctuated in parallel with her health. A letter which suffered several significant erasures reached Lady Duncannon in Italy in March or April 1792:

> I wrote to you in rather good spirits yesterday . . . for I like the quiet of this spot and E. seem'd much better and I wrote in the *morning* . . . But now I am just returned from a long solitary walk on the beach. Night silence solitude and the sea combined will unhinge the cheerfulness of anyone . . . There never has been any part of your letters that have won my attention and interested me so much as when you have appeared earnestly solicitous to convey to my mind the faith and hope and the religious confidence which I do believe exist in yours. [He recalls the Channel passage made with Elizabeth at the time of the elopement] . . . What times and what changes have passed . . . What has the interval of my life been, and what is left me – but misery from memory and a horror of reflexion!

Elizabeth's baby was born on 30 March and christened Mary on 27 April. Then in May a letter to Tom's tutor Dr Parr explained:

> . . . I have been much occupied by the state of Mrs Sheridan's health. She is going to [the Hot Wells at] Bristol. A week ago we thought there was nothing to apprehend. I leave town to follow her, for I can put nothing in competition with my feelings for her. Pray, my dear Sir, talk quietly to Tom on the subject, and desire him to write to her . . .

Sheridan was to have let one week go by before following her to Bristol, but on 2 May 'she was so sunk and alarmed' that she begged him not to leave her. So, summarily concluding his affairs in town, he set off immediately and overtook her on the road. Together they then proceeded to Bristol with 'the friend she loves best in the world', Mrs Canning, making a third. This excellent woman had put her children in charge of others, in order to perform this latest mournful kindness. At one stage earlier, her disapproval of Elizabeth's recent conduct had left her 'cooled and changed', and it had been left to Sheridan to persuade her to renew her friendship, since, he said, there was no chance of saving Elizabeth's life except by 'tranquillizing her mind'. 'She is an angel,' he insisted; 'it is all my fault.' 'God never form'd a better heart;' Elizabeth had 'no errors but what are the faults of those whose conduct has created them in her against her nature'. He must surely have meant Fitzgerald and himself.

Sometimes the patient's condition allowed hope. She drank the waters and was driven twice a day up to Kingsdown, past the very spot where, in the second of the duels he fought with Mathews twenty years before, Sheridan had been badly wounded. To Georgiana Devonshire he wrote:

I remember every thought that passed then in my mind, believing as I did that I was dying . . . I looked at the carriage that bore her down the same road, and it wrung my heart . . . My nerves are shook to pieces. The irregularity of my life and pursuits, the restless contriving temper with which I have persevered in wrong pursuits and passions makes [here are obliterations] . . . God bless you, T.L.

On the evening of 13 May Elizabeth 'desired to be placed at the piano-forte. – Looking like a shadow of her own picture [Mrs Sheridan as St Cecilia, by Reynolds] she played some notes, with tears dropping on her arms. Her mind is become heavenly, but her mortal form is fading from my sight . . . I mean to send for my son and she wishes for him.'

She was thirty-seven. When she became fully aware that she was dying, she asked the doctor for laudanum (which he gave her) so that, she said, she would not 'struggle'. She then took solemn leave of her son Tom and niece Betty Tickell. 'Your brother', so Mrs Canning wrote to Lissy Lefanu, 'behaved most wonderfully, though his heart was breaking, and at times his feelings were so violent, I feared he would be quite ungovernable at the last.' Finally, on the night of 27–28 June, Mrs Canning and Sheridan sat up throughout (as indeed Sheridan had for several nights before), he summoning up 'courage to kneel at the bedside, till he felt the last pulse . . . She died at five o'clock in the morning.' At the funeral in Wells Cathedral, 'at the last moment' Mrs Canning 'perceived a wildness in his eye' which she said terrified her, but 'it soon passed away'. They returned to London together, with Tom and little three-month-old Mary. A new tutor engaged for Tom, William Smyth, tells how at this time Sheridan would linger long by the baby's cot, trying to amuse her. And Michael Kelly, the Irish operatic tenor who was to be closely associated with Sheridan and Drury Lane over the coming years, is not the only witness to testify to Sheridan's shaken spirits in the days following his wife's death. 'I never beheld more poignant grief,' Kelly writes; 'I have seen him, night after night, cry like a child.' Sadly it was grief intensified by remorse.

He agreed with Fitzgerald to treat the child as his own. For his part, Fitzgerald hardly seems to have been overwhelmed by melancholy, still less tortured by self-accusation. 'I am afraid I have given her very unhappy moments,' he wrote to his mother, 'but on the whole more happy ones.' Being now dead, she was 'happier, much happier than any of us here. Why should one repine?' People blamed him, he said; 'according to the opinion of the world I have injured Sheridan,' but 'I must own I do not feel guilty . . . I am sorry Sheridan feels it; but I do think the story being known is his fault, not mine.' He was certain, however, that Sheridan would 'behave generously' and that 'any directions the dear angel has left he will, I am sure, fulfil with exactness'. One of these was that the education of the child should be left exclusively in Mrs Canning's hands.

More wretchedness was soon to follow. Sheridan, his son Tom, some of Tom's friends, and the Canning family were all together at Wanstead 'when the alarm was given', as Mrs Canning wrote, 'that the dear little angel was dying! It is impossible to describe the confusion and horror of the scene – Sheridan was quite frantic.' He worried at first that the baby had perhaps been mismanaged and, until the funeral, was continually in the room with it, 'indulging the sad remembrance' of mother and child. 'He suffers deeply and secretly,' said Mrs Canning, 'and I dare say he will long and bitterly lament.'

Accounts that tell of Sheridan within a short time behaving with all his old lively spirit do not necessarily contradict this judgement. Neither does the fact that within a few months he seems to have contemplated a second marriage, especially when we read that it was to be with the beautiful Pamela, daughter (by Mme de Genlis) of the Duke of Orleans, 'Philippe Egalité', and that her physical resemblance to Elizabeth Sheridan in youth was reckoned to be uncanny. Further, there is a story that the dying Elizabeth had said that if Sheridan married again, it ought to be with this Pamela. But the strangest and most piquant irony is that it was not Sheridan that Pamela married. It was Lord Edward Fitzgerald.

Two months after his wife's death Sheridan wrote to Lady Duncannon:

> I exert myself in every way and avoid remembering or reflecting as much as possible, but there are thoughts and forms and sounds that haunt my heart and will not be put away.

He was plainly concerned, too, that Lady Duncannon's love for him might have cooled, or perhaps evaporated.

> You cannot write too much to me. I shall know then that you are not estranged from me . . . I will tell you all my plans and what I mean to do when I have settled things I have fortunately been forc'd to give my attention to.

Some of these 'exertions' which Sheridan busied himself with were of course parliamentary; but there were, besides, exciting developments pending at Drury Lane. 'Garrick's Drury', the building that dated from 1674, housed its last performance in June 1791 and the following year was demolished. The King's approval for the construction of a new playhouse had not been given until January 1792, and for some time the Drury Lane company played three times a week at the King's Theatre, Haymarket (the Opera House) and twice at the Little Theatre, Haymarket. The new playhouse was to be much bigger and altogether grander than the old, capable of holding an audience of some three and a half thousand, 308 in the shilling gallery, 675 in the two-shilling gallery, 800 in the pit, and 1,800 in the four tiers of boxes. The architect in charge, whom Sheridan was endlessly consulting, was Henry Holland. The cost was to be £150,000.

10

Second Drury, second Mrs Sheridan

F INANCIAL and legal tangles arising from the old Drury were complicated enough; the new one piled Pelion on Ossa. And it was far from being simply a question of a new building replacing an old one. There was, for instance, always jealously to be fought for, the vested interest of the two 'patent' theatres in their monopoly of the London winter season. Even this was not quite so straightforward as it sounds, since there was a so-called 'dormant' patent, owned at this time by Thomas Harris of Covent Garden, with whom and with the Haymarket landowner (the Duke of Bedford), Sheridan was involved in negotiations of arcane intricacy over several years. Raising the capital for the new playhouse presented a relatively minor worry. Sheridan's gift for raising money was in any case undoubted; his troubles would always arise when it came to repaying or servicing the debt. These troubles moreover were vastly worsened by the cost of the new building being underestimated by some £75,000. The consequences in overdrafts, trust deeds, and threats from creditors, lawyers, and eventually sheriff's men, made life for Sheridan over the coming years an ever-recurring financial nightmare.

Drury Lane, properly managed, was generally judged to offer sound prospects, and the original £150,000 was successfully raised in 300 debentures of £500 each. The new theatre, it was

Drury Lane theatre as it looked in the year that Sarah Siddons made her
début there.

estimated, ought to show an annual income of between £60,000 and £75,000. In the event it seldom did, though it occasionally hit a money-spinner like Sheridan's own *Pizarro* in 1799. Sometimes the figure fell as low as £50,000. The consequence was that Sheridan's ability to pay his staff and performers punctually was destined to remain what it had always been, a close-run thing. '*Tomorrow* was always his favourite pay-day,' said his friend and admirer, Michael Kelly.

A whole company of Italian opera singers once refused to appear, because of non-payment. Even Sarah Siddons, who was a shareholder and was paid more regularly than most, complained of the difficulty in getting her money (which was £20 a night). 'Very few of the actors are paid,' she grumbled in November 1796, 'and all are threatening to withdraw themselves, yet still we go on.' Mrs Jordan, contracted to appear at 30 guineas a week, presented the management with a variety of problems. As the Duke of Clarence's mistress she might expect, and probably received, tactful treatment. Sheridan was said to be afraid of her. On the other hand her almost perpetual state of pregnancy made casting her something of a lottery. More in pleading than rebuke Sheridan begged her in December 1796 not to fail appearing in Steele's *The Conscious Lovers*: 'equal justice must be done and equal good-will shown by all the performers – or it is impossible the unprecedented high salaries of this company can be continued.' However, after playing in Shakespeare on 5 December she does not seem to have appeared again that month, and even her salary too was then in arrears.

So was that of the other principal comedy actress, Elizabeth Farren, currently the Earl of Derby's mistress and the following year to become his Countess. Without notice on 29 November, with Sheridan busy in the House of Commons, she declined to appear: 'the dirtiest trick', he protested, 'Farren has ever yet play'd . . . I found a note from her which I have answer'd and as harshly as I could. – Getting her £400 by tomorrow is out of the question.' John Kemble himself, the deputy-manager, was not exempt from these deprivations; indeed he once suffered the indignity of being arrested for debt. Resigning in umbrage in May 1796, by September he was re-engaged as actor only (at £24 a week), and by November he had succeeded in settling arrangements for payments of arrears.

The particular acuteness of Sheridan's affairs at that time arose partly from the recent death, after years of declining faculties, of Thomas Linley. Sheridan, acting in financial association with one of the closest of his friends, Joseph Richardson, and with the lawyer John Grubb (both of whom now for a time became Drury Lane co-managers with him), succeeded – *just* succeeded, after some very hectic weeks indeed – in raising enough money to pay Garrick's executors '£10,951, the principal and interest on Linley's mortgage'. So delighted was Sheridan at this final extinguishing of the Garrick 'incumbrance' that he wrote optimistically to Grubb: 'Since the final tho' long retarded enrolment of the trust-deed rely on it nothing can hurt us. I want *tomorrow* to advertise for every claim – and I will pledge my life and honour on not one difficulty or discredit remaining in a month.' Alas, very soon after this some of his most desperate rearguard actions against bankers and bailiffs were to follow.

Thomas Moore said that when Sheridan was at last obliged to make a payment, he always contrived to make it seem like a gift. And of anecdotes about him such as the following, told by Hazlitt, there are enough to fill a volume:

> Once when a creditor brought him a bill for payment, which had often been presented before, and the man complained of its soiled and tattered state, 'I'll tell you what I'd advise you to do, my friend,' said Sheridan, 'take it home and write it upon parchment.'

The trouble with him was that he easily caught the happy-go-lucky financial habits of his friends without the security of their resources. Such a one as Fox, having been first rescued from ruin by a wealthy, fond, and perhaps foolish father, was glad enough to accept salvation a second time through the subscription of his friends. (How would Fox take it? one of them wondered; why, *quarterly*, came the realistic reply.) Georgiana Devonshire's sad later years – she died in 1806 – were one long cry for help from Coutts the banker and others. But Sheridan, at least until he was approaching sixty, remained too proudly independent to sponge on his friends. In fact, when in 1808 some of them did undertake to sort out his debts, they found them, by the aristocratic standards of their day, not very large – and outweighed by bogus claims against him.

Sheridan would prefer to overlook, or perhaps simply lose, importunate demands for payment; to outwit duns and bailiffs if it came to that; and, when resources of delay were at an end, bring into play his reserves of ingenuity or guile or charm to spirit the necessary cash apparently out of thin air. If some unexpected windfall of £500 came his way, he would straightway go out and spend £600 or £1,000 – or perhaps decide to take out a lease on another house, though he already had two. He was out of Bruton Street before Elizabeth's death; then, after it, he rented one house in Lower Grosvenor Street and another, 'a large cottage', at Wanstead a little way out of London, for a time yet retaining his mansion by the Thames at Isleworth. He had house-mania much as the Duchess of Devonshire had faro-mania. Before long he had left Lower Grosvenor Street for Hertford Street, this time buying a house there for £4,000.

The new Drury Lane had opened with a flourish on 21 April 1794. The play was Kemble's version of *Macbeth*. A prologue, spoken by Kemble himself, who of course also played the title role, was written by Sheridan's old friend Fitzpatrick. An epilogue by Colman was spoken by Elizabeth Farren.

By this time Britain had been at war with revolutionary France for more than a year, and victories were hard to come by. So, naturally, when the veteran Admiral Earl Howe succeeded off Ushant in sinking the naval escort of a convoy of grain on the way from America to France, Sheridan within a few weeks was putting on a patriotic musical show in celebration: *The Glorious First of June*. (The name has stuck.) The suitably near-veteran

Palmer, the first Joseph Surface, played the piece's brave Commodore, the singers Nancy Storace and Thomas Sedgwick the heroine and hero. (Nancy Storace had been the original Susanna in Mozart's *The Marriage of Figaro*.) At least some of the lines and lyrics were by Sheridan himself. It was very much the same kind of topical entertainment that had given birth, two or three French wars before, to *Rule Britannia* and *Heart* (or in the 1794 text *Hearts*) *of Oak*. Indeed the final scene, in which the hero is sentenced to a ducking in the excellent Commodore's honour, harked directly and unashamedly back to the stirring song first sung by Garrick's Drury Lane company when the Quiberon Bay engagement of 1759 had just rounded off the elder Pitt's 'year of victories':

Commodore. Victory! Victory! – 'Hearts of Oak are our Ships – Hearts of Oak are our men'. Let me see the brave fellows. *Sailors.* Heaven bless you, noble commodore. Huzza! Huzza! Huzza! . . .

It certainly was not high art, but it hit the popular mood and taste, and it made play with all the new theatre's up-to-date stage machinery. Moreover, it could always be taken out of the cupboard, dusted down, and given a new title for the next big naval victory – as it was in three years' time, when it became *Cape St Vincent, or British Valour Triumphant*.

The 'Glorious First of June' was in 1794, rather more than a year after the outbreak of war between France and Britain, and five years after the event which had marked for Englishmen the beginning of revolution in France. Sheridan had greeted the fall of the Bastille as enthusiastically as Fox himself. At a meeting held to celebrate its first anniversary in 1790 it had been Sheridan who proposed the motion 'That this meeting does most cordially rejoice in the establishment and confirmation of liberty in France'. Indeed his excessive zeal in proposing it was said to have embarrassed some of his friends present. He became a member of Grey's rather narrowly aristocratic 'Society of the Friends of the People'; supported also Grey's abortive 1793 bill proposing parliamentary reform; and in the Commons politely but trenchantly ridiculed Burke's apocalyptic prophecies of anarchy and tyranny and his calls for an anti-French, anti-revolutionary crusade. Then, when war came, he made a strong and scornful attack on the witch-hunt against reformers that he claimed Pitt and his Home Secretary Dundas were busy promoting. Had 'patriots in pot-houses' actually dared to transmit friendly addresses to the National Convention in Paris? – what a heinous crime! And then there was 'Mr Hardy, an honest shoemaker' (this was Thomas Hardy, of the London Corresponding Society, which advocated universal male suffrage); little had he dreamt, 'God help him, how near he had been to overturning the constitution'.

Through 1793 and 1794 Sheridan continued to attack measures against the supposed seditious practices of radicals alleged to be in sympathy with the enemy or stirring up popular discontent, in particular two Scotsmen, the unitarian Thomas Palmer and the lawyer Thomas Muir, who were, despite his efforts to save them, convicted to seven and fourteen years' transportation respectively. (Palmer, he asserted, had merely advocated parliamentary reform in words remarkably like those used earlier by the Duke of Richmond and Pitt himself.) 'Good God, sir,' Sheridan exclaimed, 'is it possible that this can be the law of Scotland?' In much the same spirit four years later, Sheridan together with Fox and an influential group of Whig friends, energetically assisted – this time successfully – the defence at Maidstone Assizes of Arthur O'Connor, an associate of Elizabeth's lover Fitzgerald and involved with him in the tragic Irish troubles of 'ninety-eight'. (O'Connor was acquitted; Fitzgerald, under arrest, died of wounds.) Without positively siding with the rebels, Sheridan's words in Parliament implied basic sympathy with them: 'To keep Ireland against the will of the people is a vain expectation. With 80,000 troops against an unarmed and undisciplined multitude, is it not clear that the contest lies between the government and the people? . . . The fair presumption is that the government is to blame.' Again, in Parliament two years later, he fought hard but of course unsuccessfully against Pitt's Act of Union which abolished the Dublin Parliament.

Sheridan had sided emphatically with Fox when the break came with Burke and he would have no truck with the drift towards Pitt which by 1793 had enlisted a majority of the once-Foxite Whigs under the banner of the administration. But neither would he go all the way with Fox, whose anti-war stance was unshakeable. Sheridan could still exclaim in 1794 that 'any minister ought to be impeached and lose his head who spilled the blood of his countrymen . . . to restore the ancient despotism of France'. But those last half-dozen words were the important ones. A war *to defend British traditions and liberties*, a war against aggressive and murderous foreign tyrants, would be another matter. More and more as the years went by he became conventionally, patriotically, and even militantly anti-French, though as late as 1795 he still felt able to support a petition for peace negotiations presented in the Commons.

Two years later, when there were naval mutinies at the Nore and Spithead, he was sure where his loyalties ought to lie. Refusing to make party capital out of the crisis, he suffered the pain of being praised by Pitt for his 'fair, candid, and liberal conduct'. Pitt remained anathema to him, and to be applauded by Pitt for 'merely doing his duty when he spoke of the sailors' made him, he said, almost ashamed. Many times he went out of his way to stress that in general he still stood by Fox (who as repeatedly told his friends how much he doubted it – Sheridan, he complained, 'itched to be different'); but refusing as he did meekly to accept Fox's line as a matter of course meant that a certain mistrust of him, originating perhaps as long ago as the regency crisis, now took stronger hold in the minds of Fox and his small band of faithful followers. When Fox in his frustration led his parliamentary troops away to boycott the Commons for a time, Sheridan did reluctantly go with them, but he was not happy sulking with Achilles in his tent, and by the spring of 1798, with Bonaparte threatening invasion, he made a strongly unFoxite speech. Yes, he declared, he *had* rejoiced in the establishment of a republic in France, but he deplored the 'scenes of blood which stained its glorious efforts to be free' and now everything possible must be done to defend against the French 'the sinews and the bones . . . the marrow and the very heart's blood of Great Britain'. As for the attitude of 'some gentlemen', he found it childish; for was it not childish to say, 'I will wait till the enemy have landed and then I will resist them?'

In April 1795 Sheridan married Hester Jane, youngest of the four daughters of Newton Ogle, Dean of Winchester. To Sheridan she was to be 'Hecca', his 'heart's Hecca', 'dear Wench', his 'own Gipsey', his 'dear bit of brown Holland'. And with her, 'Sheridan' was to lose its first two syllables and become 'Dan', a name he happily adopted, often using it in the 'third person playful': 'Think kindly of poor Dan'; 'Dan loves you more and more a thousand times and you shall see there shall be an end of the least cause of Hecca's fretting.'

For fretting of course there was to be – was bound to be in anyone married to one such as Sheridan, constantly separated from his wife by parliamentary or Drury Lane business, seldom free for long of some theatrical, financial, or personal crisis, never in one place for more than a day or two at a time, chronically liable to drink too much, always forgetting or otherwise missing appointments, 'apt to eat the calf in the cow's belly' (it was her phrase), regularly penitent, ever incorrigible. Nobody of course would have married Sheridan expecting a life of uneventful domesticity, and naturally Hester Ogle did not. She was a lively girl from a well-to-do family, clerical on both sides; used to comfortable living; reckoning to enjoy a married life of social standing and perhaps some display. She required to be able to dress in the fashion, or better still a little daringly ahead of it. (A year or two after the wedding, obviously indignant at some hostile criticism of her, Sheridan wrote that *certainly* there 'was nothing but what was perfectly proper and decent' in her dress; and, a little later again, she was credited by the *Morning Herald* with being 'the inventor of a fashionable new cloak'.) She was a tolerable singer, a good dancer, and a horse-rider bold enough to attract in the first years of the marriage several nervous warnings from her husband. If a brother of hers bought one of the smart, speedy new curricles, she must drive it and tell her absent Dan how skilful she was at it. Though her tastes were expensive, so of course were Sheridan's own, not least in marrying her at all – his friends were astonished that he was able to raise the large settlement insisted on by the Dean. It was far from 'fretting' all the time. Middle-aged as her bridegroom was, more than double her own age (of not quite twenty), he was a famous public figure, and still a charmer, despite a bottle-scarred complexion and a nose whose redness had by now become every cartoonist's cliché. Impossible as he was, and though more than once she was seriously to contemplate a separation from him, she was still able to tell Lord Holland, after seventeen years of marriage, 'My whole heart and soul is with Sheridan.'

In the years after the wedding he became squire of Polesden, near Bookham and Box Hill in what the *Morning Chronicle* called 'a prime and sporting part of Surrey'. The estate included the seventeenth-century mansion of Polesden Lacey, pleasure grounds, lands, and farms, in all 341 acres, and the price he paid (£12,384) was not much different from the cost of the marriage settlement the year before. Sheridan promised his wife:

. . . we shall have the nicest place within a prudent distance from town in England. And sweet Hecca shall have a horse after her own fancy, and it shall be the seat of health and happiness – where she shall chirp like a bird, bound like a fawn and grow fat as a little pig . . . The thought and plan of this . . . puts all dismal thoughts from me

– in contrast with Bath, where he had recently been on theatre business and every memory had conspired to make him 'lemoncholy as a yew-tree in a churchyard'.

As a gentleman-farmer and lord of the manors of Polesden Lacey and West Humble, Sheridan took on added status but also new responsibilities and some new worries to add to his already substantial load – quarrels over enclosures of common land; arguments over timber-felling rights; disputes with tenant-farmers over rent payments; anxiety about the weather at harvest time, or perhaps about shortage of money (as in 1798) 'to wind up my harvest'; even fretting over the house's exposure to the east wind, which he feared earlier that year might be too bitter for his 'soul's own Hecca' – she should come to London, where he had 'constant fires prepared'.

The purchase of Polesden was contractually linked with the marriage settlement, and trustees were appointed, one of whom was Samuel Whitbread, the wealthy brewer and Whig politician. The other was Charles Grey, who more than once in the Sheridan story appears as a man of influence befriending Hester and trying to safeguard her interests. In 1808 we find Sheridan writing in indignation to his lawyer about payments involved in the purchase of neighbouring farms – he was always scheming to expand and improve his Surrey empire:

> I don't comprehend what is meant by the trustees having taken possession of the two farms. They can have no possession but as in trust for me – and subject to my right to manage my own estate under the marriage settlements, securing them Mrs S's pinmoney . . . I am greatly surprised at your saying yesterday that *under the trust* the whole estate *must be sold* at my death. I have taken care by my will that not an acre of it shall be parted with . . . and it must be most clumsy management indeed if after the additional purchases I have made it will not amply provide for my wife's jointure and that upon real security . . .

Not content merely with incorporating contiguous farmlands

into his estate, he also for a time rented Randall Farm at neighbouring Leatherhead and used it as an auxiliary country retreat. It was from there in September 1808 that the following 'summons' was sent to one of his friends:

> . . . You are hereby charged and required to be personally present . . . at eleven of the clock on Monday morning next, in order that you may be present at a fishing festival on the banks of the river Mole and that you be aiding and assisting in hauling the nets and tackle . . . whereof on your allegiance fail not . . .

There were shooting parties too. Amid the enjoyments of one of them he dispatches one of his innumerable notes to the Drury Lane treasurer in which, after first promising to *crush* a certain Hosier, one of the theatre's trustees, he writes: 'As we say of our troops, I am in high health and spirits.' But then: 'I am undone for want of £35 – I trust I shall have it by to-morrow's coach that I may get to town Tuesday.'

Although he was seldom to stay at Polesden for many weeks at a time, it was always to remain his main country property. When he was over sixty with not long to live, he was even planning to rebuild the 'ruin' which by then he considered he had paid a 'shameful price' for. He proposed to build a new house 'of taste and convenience', lay out the grounds, repair the farms, and thus improve the estate so that 'if it were to come to sale' its value would be 40 per cent bettered. Then, never one for understatement, he crossed out *forty* and wrote *fifty*. Already by that time he was anxious to silence the rumour that at Polesden he had bitten off more than he could chew.

Through these years at the close of the century the speeches of the honourable member for Stafford sounded mellifluously and often weightily over the Commons benches; the pleasantries and witticisms of Mr Sheridan rang brightly at Brooks's and in the drawing rooms of St James's or Devonshire House or Woburn; the style maintained by the proprietor of Hertford Street and

[161]

The second Mrs Sheridan ('Hecca') and her son Charles: an engraving by H. Meyer after Joshua Reynolds.

Polesden Lacey was of the best. But the numerous and frequently frantic scrawls hurriedly dispatched by the manager of Drury Lane to his treasurer there, Richard Peake, who was the nightly taker of the receipts providing the only means of keeping the Sheridan show on the road – in effect the keeper of his privy purse – present a picture in such contrast as to be almost grotesque:

Dec. 1797: If you have not another pound in the house you must give me twenty guineas of my money this night.

Feb. 1798, Star and Garter, Pall Mall: Send me pray two pound or I shall be stuck here for my reckoning.

Aug. 1799?: Pray pawn your credit once more for me, and send me . . . a six dozen hamper of good wine, viz. 4 dozen port and two dozen sherry, and that will set me up.

Dec. 1799, Shakespeare's Head Tavern, Covent Garden: You must positively come to me here, and bring £60 in your pocket – Fear nothing. Be civil to all claimants, for trust me in three months there will not exist one unsatisfied claimant. Shut up the office and come here directly.

[*1799–1800*]: If you stop the first carriage or knock down the first man that goes past your door you must give the bearer of this ten pounds. It is really a matter of almost life and death . . .

May 1800: *Without fail* and immediately give the bearer 5 guineas to buy hay and corn for my coach horses – they have not had a morsel of either since last night.

[*1801?*]: Pray hasten the wine and add sherry to it or we are all aground –

Such scribbled notes as these, and there are very many of them, may be set beside the letters written over roughly the same period to his young wife in her early and middle twenties. These by turns are playful, apologetic, self-justifying, self-excusing; solicitous for her health or safety; tumbling over with well-meaning promises and tender endearments. Reading between their lines, one may perceive easily enough signs of strains and differences present or ahead. But the marriage carried blessings too, one of the earliest of these the birth in January 1796 of a second son for Sheridan – Charles, but at first usually 'Robin' to his father. The elder boy Tom was by then twenty, nearly the same age as Hecca. To both Tom and Charles, Sheridan was always to be an unfailingly devoted father.

A thousand thanks my own dear Wench for your letter just arrived – Hecca's kind words make Dan glad . . . O give sweet Robin a quantity of kisses for me.

. . . Heart of mine – I have only a moment to bless you – and again to beg no risks [in horse-riding] . . . I shall not see my soul's love till Friday.

. . . O my heart's light and life there is nothing makes amends for these absences and at times all my fits of nervous gloom come over me – for want of my angel Hecca to brush them off with her soft white wings . . .

. . . Well my heart I will not fail to be at Midhurst tomorrow at six. These vile politics shall not keep me . . . Be careful sweet love . . .

. . . I shall settle everything yet – and we will be comfortable and separate no more – . . .

Wooburn, Friday night: My pretty Wench, now are you fast asleep – and your arm under one of your rosy cheeks . . . I have millions to say to you but why do you not write my Hecca?

. . . My soul's beloved, I know your green eyes will grieve when I tell you it is indispensably necessary for me to go to town . . .

. . . My dear Wench I do long to see thy eyes. Betsy told me you look remarkably well and certainly fatter which rejoiced the cockles of Dan's heart. You never tell me anything about yourself or Robin or . . . or or or – Kiss my child for me.

Sheridan, at Polesden, was in anguish when 'Robin', at the age of six, caught scarlet fever. There was a dangerous epidemic of it in the neighbourhood, and several in his household were stricken, with two of the maids 'extremely bad'. The boy was for a time thought to be dying, while Hester too was ill and Sheridan himself was afflicted with bladder irritation and a fever – though he recovered in time to go the following month to Stafford and be elected once more, again unopposed. Bringing down to Polesden his own doctor, Andrew Bain, who had attended his first wife, and William Fraser, who was physician extraordinary to the Prince of Wales, he instructed Peake to send Fraser £50 immediately from Drury Lane and another £50 urgently to Polesden, 'on my son's sickness . . . I will answer it', he promised, 'to the Chancellor.' For by this time Drury Lane's affairs had been made subject to orders from the Court of Chancery.

Constantly through the first decade of his second marriage, the affairs of the theatre, and of Sheridan himself as principal proprietor and manager, were under siege from creditors and bankers, and sometimes very uncomfortably from bailiffs too. (A bailiff in occupation once at Byron's told him, 'My Lord, I have been in Mr Sheridan's twelve month at a time – a civil gentleman – knows how to deal with us.') Sheridan was frequently at odds with the theatre's trustees who in 1799 filed a bill against him for violating the 1793 deed which guaranteed them the first £40 of every night's takings. He promised them to make good the deficiency, but five years later the trustees were still complaining: in 1804 they threatened that if *arrears of £16,000* were not paid within one month, the management would be placed 'in other hands'. In between these two occasions Sheridan and his associate, John Grubb, were required several times to answer in Chancery for their debts. Court records of 1801 moreover show that in February of that year a writ was issued by the Court of the Exchequer to sequester Sheridan's property until he appeared to answer charges, and in June a subpoena demanded his appearance in the Court of King's Bench in another case involving Drury Lane's finances. But at least as long as he bore the immunity of a Member of Parliament he was safe from arrest for debt.

Chancery proceedings sauntered on into 1802, a year in which Kemble was finally to break with Sheridan and afterwards take £22,000 of his money, his own shining talent, and that of his sister Sarah Siddons, over to Covent Garden; a year too in which Sheridan was to break with Grubb, who then started proceedings against him. When a climax eventually arrived in Chancery, it was Sheridan who, bringing into play his skills in oratory (and escapology) was to achieve a gratifying if temporary victory, at least succeeding in persuading the court to allow the performers' salaries to have first claim on future receipts, rather than the creditors, as they were claiming.

In the years immediately preceding these events in Chancery, and in the teeth of internal strife and incessant threats of disaster, the Drury Lane company headed by Kemble, Mrs Siddons, and Mrs Jordan enjoyed several satisfying successes, and with *Pizarro* in 1799 (however fustian it is now generally deemed) one resounding triumph.

Following the fiasco of *Vortigern*, fraudulently sold to Drury Lane as a newly discovered play by Shakespeare, there came *Castle Spectre* by the young but already celebrated Matthew 'Monk' Lewis. This was in the fashionable Gothic-romantic, ghosts-and-horror manner, and ran excellently for sixty nights. Alongside it Sheridan put on *The Stranger*, a translation from the German of Kotzebue, adapted by Sheridan himself, who also wrote the words for a song in it whose air was contributed by the Duchess of Devonshire.

The Stranger gave Mrs Siddons one of those romantic, powerful parts she was supremely good in, and the play was sufficiently successful to set Sheridan looking at a translation of another Kotzebue play, *Die Spanier in Peru*, which was itself based on Marmontel's *Les Incas* of 1777. He worked on it in the three months from December 1798 to March 1799 – he was still calling it *Rolla* then, after its leading character – some of this time hiding away from trouble at an inn, The Black Dog, between Hounslow and Staines. Towards the end of March he was writing from there to his wife:

Sunday. Here am I, my beloved Hecca, at my little *Inn* after writing all the rainy part of the morning and walking seven miles on the Heath during two fine hours . . . *Wednesday* . . . I have been going over Rolla with Kemble . . . All the scenery, dresses, and musick are going on . . . If the last line of Rolla is compleat before I go to bed I will be with you on Saturday to dinner, if not by your own green eyes on Sunday . . .

Rolla became *Pizarro, a Tragedy*, and *Pizarro* was the sensation of the season. Judged as it were in a vacuum, it must now seem – as indeed it seemed to many critical spirits then – a rather trumpery long-winded melodrama, by turns sentimental and bombastic, at times painfully resembling Mr Puff's Spanish Armada tragedy of which Sheridan had twenty years before made such delicate fun in *The Critic*. But, bad as *Pizarro* is, it must not be seen *in vacuo* but in context. It was written partly to satisfy the public appetite for dramatic spectacle, but also to reflect loyal and patriotic emotions in a nation which had passed the previous year under serious fear of invasion by Bonaparte. Heavily adapting the already translated Kotzebue, Sheridan seized every opportunity to give his tragedy not only the most lavish musical and scenic setting (de Loutherbourg again), but also an easily apprehended topical relevance. In Act 2, Scene 2, for instance, he expanded a mere three lines of Kotzebue's dialogue to fill the best part of a page of thunder-rolling rhetoric to be delivered by Rolla to his warriors before the Inca Temple of the Sun, in praise of throne and altar: 'Victory or death! our King! our Country! and our God!'

Sheridan not only reckoned on interruptions of patriotic applause at such points, but went out of his way beforehand to prompt prominent society figures like the Devonshire House ladies to lead it – and one of them, Lady Elizabeth Foster, later confirmed that 'the huge audience huzzaed at every speech or allusion to which a loyal or patriotic colour might be given'. Some

at least of this Sheridan-Rolla-Kemble 'victory or death' oration
deserves longer quotation:

Your generous spirit has compared as mine has, the motives,
which in a war like this, can animate *their* minds, and OURS.
THEY, by a strange frenzy driven, fight for power, for plunder,
and extended rule – WE, for our country, our altars, and our
homes. – THEY follow an Adventurer whom they fear – and
obey a power which they hate – WE serve a Monarch whom we
love – a God whom we adore. – Whene'er they move in anger,
desolation tracks their progress! – Where'er they pause in
amity, affliction mourns their friendship! – They boast they
come but to improve our state, enlarge our thoughts, and free
us from the yoke of error! Yes – THEY will give enlightened
freedom to *our* minds, who are themselves the slaves of
passion, avarice, and pride – They offer us their protection –
Yes, such protection as vultures give to lambs – covering and
devouring them! – They call on us to barter all of good we have
inherited and proved, for the desperate chance of something
better which they promise. – Be our plain answer this: The
Throne WE honour is the PEOPLE'S CHOICE – the laws we
reverence are our brave Fathers' legacy – the faith we follow
teaches us to live in bonds of charity with all mankind, and die
with hope of bliss beyond the grave. Tell your invaders this,
and tell them too, we seek no change; and least of all, such
change as they would bring us.
                    Trumpets sound.

It was gratifying that the King, like everyone else, came to see
Pizarro, and was reported as 'applauding very much, with taste
and judgement', but no doubt it was as well that Sheridan did not
hear the poor opinion of it he volunteered privately to Lord
Harcourt. Fox thought it 'the worst thing possible', and Pitt
merely ventured to observe, with a smile, that he recognized
some of Mr Sheridan's favourite figures that he had earlier
admired at the trial of Mr Hastings.

All in all, despite some enthusiastic contemporary verdicts, professional criticism of Sheridan's last great success has always been stern, even when Kotzebue has been made to take a big share of the blame. The harshness of this disapproval might have been softened if it could have been shown that Sheridan was writing merely with his tongue in his cheek and his eye necessarily on the box-office. This last he certainly was, but it is also obvious that he was proud of *Pizarro*. He liked rhetoric, valued it, was good at it. He enjoyed spectacle. He had never been afraid of sentiment, and by now was not too nice about laying it on with a trowel. His play, so he informed his Devonshire House friends, was 'the finest ever known'.

He dedicated it, though in language somewhat veiled and mysterious, to his wife. ('Poor Hester', wrote Mrs Bouverie, 'had suffered agonies of mind about this play, and continues as violently attached to him as ever.') He became almost as solicitous for his tragedy's well-being as for his boy Charles's* – anxious enough to be unusually attentive to preparation and rehearsal, worried by what he considered Mrs Jordan's inadequacy as Cora, and not always quite satisfied even with Mrs Siddons as Elvira. Only with Kemble's Rolla was he entirely delighted: 'Nothing ever equalled that!' he exclaimed, clapping his hands like a child.

As usual, before the first night there were irritations, delays, frustrations, arguments, rewritings, and several postponements. Michael Kelly, *Pizarro*'s musical director, relates that even on the first night Sheridan was still adding to some fifth-act speeches backstage while the first act was being played. With the drama's crowded action, overblown dialogue, interludes of music (both solos and choruses), scenic effects, and ambitious spectacle, the first performance did not end till five minutes before midnight, and the cuts then judged to be imperative knocked

---

* He not only consciously associated Cora's (Mrs Jordan's) child in the drama with his own young son, but when a painting of Kemble, commissioned by Sheridan, was exhibited at the Royal Academy in 1800 he was shown holding Sheridan's little three-year-old.

eighty minutes off the running time. But Sheridan, like Puff in *The Critic* ('Egad, I'll print it every word!'), published the work in full and very remuneratively: it ran through twenty-one impressions in its first six months.

As a guest again at a Whig party at Woburn, Sheridan was greeted, but not abashed, by some adverse opinions of his tragedy. As to the theatrical judgment of Fox or Fitzpatrick, he said, he would 'as lief talk to a shoemaker'. Later, at Devonshire House, when Lady Melbourne also criticized the play, Sheridan came back to her with, 'God denied you a poetic mind. You are fit only to pick out the eyes of potatoes by the dozen.' Then, after dinner, he turned to flirting with Lady Elizabeth Foster in *Pizarro* terms: 'O that you would come, O Péruvienne, with me!' – 'very tender,' she reflected comfortably, 'but very entertaining'.

The profits from *Pizarro*'s long run, while handsome, were very far from being sufficient to clear the debts of Drury Lane or its proprietors. By 1800 the sheriff's men were in possession at Hertford Street, and one of them, a bailiff named Postan, is the authority for a Sheridan story which has at least a measure of trustworthiness in the feel of it. Making his clearance, the bailiff offered to spare any single article for which Sheridan had 'a sentiment or a necessity'. To his surprise Sheridan led him up to the library, and took from a shelf 'an old battered folio'. 'It belonged to my father,' he explained. It was – so the anecdote alleges – a *first edition* of Shakespeare. Perhaps a cynic might conclude that he was merely showing shrewd appreciation of the future movement of book values. But whether it was really a first, or merely an old, edition, what seems most probable is that he was indulging an honest sentiment and wishing to remember his crotchety old father with piety.

Out of Hertford Street, he was a wanderer in London for a year or two before once more coming to rest, this time in George Street, Hanover Square.

There was to be no more playwriting. Michael Kelly once suggested to him the real reason: he was too afraid, afraid of the author of *The School for Scandal*. Sheridan did not disagree. Of course that master-comedy was still frequently put on, and one particular performance of it made a very special occasion. It was in May 1802, and notable for two reasons: it marked the first appearance as Lady Teazle of the delightful Mrs Jordan – still at the age of forty a huge favourite – and the final appearance of the actor who had been prominent on the London stage for half a century, the first Sir Peter Teazle, the original Mr Puff, Thomas King. After curtain-fall there were scenes of devotion and tribute. Mrs Jordan had not allowed her acting career to suffer excessive interference from her position as mistress to the royal Duke of Clarence and already the mother of seven of his children. Primarily a performer in comedy, though she was versatile and a good singer as well, her sparkle and vivacity long captivated the Drury Lane audience. Leigh Hunt, no mean judge, reckoned her the first actress of her day, even ahead of the not easily comparable Mrs Siddons.

Another outstanding Drury Lane occasion was to come two years later, with the 'Master Betty' phenomenon. William Betty, alias 'the young Roscius', the boy prodigy (he was thirteen but still played Hamlet), was having such sensational success that his backers were demanding fifty guineas a night for him. At first Drury Lane demurred, and Covent Garden snapped him up. But Sheridan was determined not to miss this immense box-office attraction. 'Should he be engaged for the 12 nights at Covent Garden your next step must be to have him pursued to Liverpool,' he instructed his representative, 'and engage him for 12 nights for us on the same terms.' Dining with the boy, he found him bashful – astonishingly so in view of his confidence facing an audience. Certainly he was 'something extraordinary and the manner people flock after him equally so'. 'He is the most lovely creature that ever was seen,' he told Hester, 'and the most unlike any other human that ever I saw.' The Master Betty boom was profitable for the short time it lasted, with takings of £600 a night, but twelve performances were hardly sufficient significantly to affect the depressed financial predicament either of

Drury Lane or of its principal proprietor.

The Sheridan of *Pizarro*, the loyal patriot, was often in evidence again in the years following his play's big success. When in 1800 an attempt was made on George III's life while he, with the Queen and some of the Princesses, attended a Drury Lane performance, Sheridan was again in the limelight. While the King moved to the front of the royal box to demonstrate that he had not been hit, Sheridan, by means of an innocent deception, contrived to keep the Queen and Princesses calm in the background and later helped to remove and interrogate the would-be assassin. 'The King says he never can forget Sheridan's attention,' wrote Georgiana Devonshire to her mother, 'especially in breaking it as he did to the princesses.' Then, when the time came for the National Anthem, vociferously received, Michael Kelly found that Sheridan's quick wits and sense of occasion had devised extempore a new verse for him to sing: 'From every latent foe / From the assassin's blow/ God save the King! / O'er him thine arm extend / O Lord defend our King /Our Father, Prince, and Friend / God save the King!'

Sheridan's oration in December 1802 on the Army Estimates was one of the most powerful and brilliant of his whole career, however 'foolish' Fox rated it. To hear it, Hester went to the Strangers' Gallery dressed as a man. Then when invasion once again threatened in the following year, Sheridan was very active, in the Commons and outside, in support of the corps of yeomanry and volunteers, rejoicing 'to find that a military disposition pervaded the land'. He even became commander of the St James's Volunteers himself, and was pleased to find himself in August 1803 received with the utmost affability by the King, who greatly astonished him not only by the way 'he picked up everything', but in particular by knowing about an accident Hester had just sustained in dancing, and indeed by speaking 'a great deal' on this same subject of dancing. The Queen's corns, he confided, 'had providentially interfered with her early propensity to become a proficient in that frivolous and often mischievous accomplishment'. It was hardly the sort of conversation the King would have been likely to have with Fox.

Among some undated letters in the collected *Correspondence of George Prince of Wales* there are four to the Prince from the second Mrs Sheridan which are painfully eloquent of her domestic plight at the time of writing. At least one of them from the address given must date from 1806, but it is fair to suppose that one, or perhaps more, of them belong to 1803, for in April of that year Charles Grey was writing:

> I went last night by her desire to see Mrs Sheridan. She had nobody to attend on her but her maid. They have not a silver fork or teaspoon left, and she was obliged to send to buy a bottle of wine at a tavern for wine and water. In short, if I was to enter into a detail of her wretchedness I should never finish.

The letters to the Prince are certainly those of a woman in desperation:

> Saturday. I had troubled your Royal Highness with a letter expressive of the horror of my situation. I have burnt it – I have troubled you enough. Only let me entreat that I may enter the house you so graciously offer'd me immediately – I can bear this no longer. Sheridan's treatment of me is inconceivable, is infamous. I beseech you, Sir, to let me find a shelter in that house . . .

The next two may be from about the same time, but the Devonshire House reference argues perhaps a rather later date:

> Thursday night. I implore your Royal Highness to see me a few moments tomorrow . . . I fear I have been the cause of mischief where I would sacrifice myself a thousand times

rather than be so. There is *nothing* the people at D. House would not do to injure S. if they could. I alas! am the cause of it, but you, Sir, *must* feel the difference of *their* attachment and his. Only hear me, but for God's sake do not to them or to him speak of it. Will your Royal Highness be in the Park tomorrow? . . . Do not, Sir, think me mad . . . I will wait for your Royal Highness in the street – I will do anything . . . Tuesday. Poor Sheridan's mind appears in so agitated a state just now that I cannot help troubling your Royal Highness with one word . . . When I have an opportunity I will repeat to you, Sir, a conversation I had with him the other night which shock'd me more than I have words to express. His drinking lately has been entirely owing to the state of his spirits – I am sure of it.

The existence of a severe domestic crisis at about midsummer 1803 is confirmed by an equally desperate-sounding letter from Sheridan to his wife, eloquent of his own misery. They had been married eight years.

By my life and soul if you talk of leaving me now you will destroy me. I am wholly unwell – I neither sleep or eat. You are before my eyes night and day. I will contrive that you shall go to the North at all events, but don't leave me to myself . . . I will set out on Saturday or Sunday to come to you . . . Pray let me hear from you by return of post . . . Dear Charles kiss your mother for me, for if I live 'till you have mind to know me you will not cease to love me. Bless you Hecca. S.

There was no separation, though much of Hester's time was always to be spent at the homes of other members of her family in Kent, Sussex, Northumberland, and particularly Hampshire.

Prince of Wales's man

PITT went out of office when his proposals for removing Catholic disabilities were vetoed by the King, and from 1801 to 1804 Addington was Prime Minister. During that interval before the return of Pitt, Sheridan's unpopularity with Fox and the Foxites increased. He was suspect, 'unreliable'. He was too often and too obviously seen to be hobnobbing with Addington; and it is true that he was often ready to support and always inclined to tolerate Addington as the best alternative to Pitt. Pitt's talents were great and admitted; but he was arrogant; he was a 'rogue'; he was always the prime enemy. 'Pitt attack'd me,' wrote Sheridan to his Hecca, in jocular-bucolic; 'and Dan he trim him I assure you.' Much was in a state of flux on the domestic political scene at this time, but Sheridan's dislike of Pitt was constant as the north star.

The time-honoured separation of eighteenth-century politicans simply into Whigs and Tories was never adequate to describe mid-Georgian political realities, and for those opening years of the nineteenth century it makes only very limited sense. Contemporary party managers and students of political connections would rather be thinking in terms of Pittites, Foxites, 'Addingtons', 'Grenvilles', a handful of 'Prince of Wales's Friends', some 'uncertains', and many independents. Party whips and party discipline lay far into the future, and although

Sheridan would always in the broad sense of the word consider himself a Whig, he might reasonably be counted as now belonging at the same time to the Foxites (if only residually), to the Prince's party (increasingly, until later his very tenure of a seat depended on the Prince's backing), and, most emphatically of all, to the independents. Time and again he stressed that he would speak his own mind, and not hold himself bound by party ties or obligations to the Prince of Wales. Frequent participation in the junketings of Carlton House and Brighton did not prevent him, for instance, from differing with the Prince at this time on two matters in particular: the Prince's request (not for the first time, and rejected by both King and government) for a military command, and the ever-recurring question of Catholic emancipation, a reform which Sheridan would always champion.

His attendance in the Commons remained regular, and he seldom failed to speak on important issues – the war, taxation, Ireland, civil liberties. And of course he often busied himself with lesser matters. We find him for instance in 1803 moving the second reading of the Surrey Iron Railway Bill. 'I am an enthusiast on the subject,' he wrote at the time, 'and a decided foe to the stupid eagerness of extending the plan of canals where they can only be mischievous, above all in our county [Surrey].' He spoke well impromptu, but on weightier questions he would often prepare careful notes, some of which survive, some even marked at the point where he planned to interject a well-timed cry of 'Good God, Mr Speaker!' or some similar orator's ploy of carefully considered spontaneity. Thomas Sheridan had once said of his son that the care he took with his speeches was exceeded only by the care he took to conceal it.

He had often maintained with reasonable pride that he never begged for a sinecure, as was then common practice. But in 1804 the Prince of Wales offered him the place of Receiver General to the Duchy of Cornwall, which, though its value fluctuated, was reckoned to be worth as much as £1,400 a year. (In fact Sheridan later insisted to his wife, with an offer of vouchers to prove the fact, that it amounted to no more than £940.) While gratefully accepting it, he went out of his way to emphasize that it would in no way tie his hands.

Then however it transpired that the Prince had overlooked an earlier promise made to one of his former equerries, General Lake, that when the place fell vacant it should go to him. But since Lake was by now in India and could not by any stretching of even sinecurist ethics be permitted to hold the post while so far distant from the Duchy, and since his brother's claim to hold it for him as deputy was rejected, Sheridan was able to accept it, though on the condition, which he volunteered, that he would resign when Lake came home. In 1807 Lake returned and Sheridan did resign. But Lake died in the following year, so the place was Sheridan's for the rest of his life. Occasionally the Duchy's accounts might receive a windfall, a percentage of which would become due to the Receiver; and Creevey, one of the Prince's cronies who saw a good deal of Sheridan and his wife at this time, tells how a particularly juicy plum once fell unexpectedly into the Receiver's lap. 'Sheridan', he writes,

> was of course very much set up with this £1,300, and, on the very next day upon leaving us, he took a house at Barnes Terrace where he spent all his £1,300. At the end of two or three months at most, the tradespeople would no longer supply him without being paid, so he was obliged to remove . . . Yet he was as full of his fun during these two months as ever he could be – gave dinners perpetually and was always on the road between Barnes and London, or Barnes and Oatlands (the Duke of York's), in a large job coach upon which he would have his family arms painted . . .

If not for himself, Sheridan *was* always ready to solicit favours for his son Tom. Creevey indeed relates how Sheridan pleaded passionately but unsuccessfully with the Prince for the Receivership to go to Tom, not himself. Tom Sheridan was like his father in many ways, lively, quick-witted, likeable, sociable, improvident. (He was blessed with the good looks of the Linleys, but cursed with their tubercular inheritance.) Sheridan had tried to give him the best of everything, a good education with tutors at Cambridge, a generous if not always punctually paid allowance, a share – eventually a quarter-share – in Drury Lane receipts. When his son became involved in a divorce case and had to find 'crim. con.' damages of £1,500, it was Sheridan who paid. In 1805 Tom eloped with an heiress, to the delight of his father, who told Creevey he found his daughter-in-law 'lovely and engaging and interesting beyond measure . . . with a most superior intelligence'. Naturally he was anxious that his son should have a seat in Parliament, and three times Tom tried unsuccessfully, twice at Liskeard and once at Stafford, which cost the Prince of Wales in all some £8,000 in election expenses on Tom's behalf.

Pitt returned as Prime Minister for twenty months, but died in January 1806, aged only forty-six, shortly after the triumph of Trafalgar and the disaster of Austerlitz. The next administration was formed from a broad coalition of Foxites (the King at last bowing to the necessity of accepting Fox), 'Grenvilles' (Lord Grenville headed the Treasury), 'Addingtons' (Addington became Lord Sidmouth), and two of the Prince of Wales's party, Lord Moira and Sheridan himself. It was not to enjoy a long life, and had little claim to be dubbed, as it was, the 'Ministry of All the Talents'.

Return to office after twenty-three consecutive years in opposition: it sounds as if this should have been the occasion for hanging out flags, and indeed Sheridan did put on a grand dinner for his friends, including the Prince of Wales – a feast intended also to celebrate the christening of a second Richard Brinsley in the family, Tom's son, Sheridan's first grandchild.* But in fact 1806 marks the beginning of the political end for him. He still had ten years to live, but they were to be years largely of disappointment, resentment, and even humiliation. At the outset he found himself passed over for a place in the Cabinet, where the Prince of

---

* Tom and his wife had in all six children. Three daughters became famous beauties of their day, Lady Dufferin, Mrs Caroline Norton, and Lady Seymour, later Duchess of Somerset.

William Pitt addressing the House of Commons, by K.A. Hickel: Fox and Sheridan are to be seen on the Opposition front bench.

Wales's interest was represented instead by Lord Moira.
Sheridan became Navy Treasurer, which if it offered little power
or prestige, at least briefly afforded him a handsome salary and an
official residence in Somerset Place.

Some of his resentment came out strongly in a letter he dashed
off to Fox in February 1806:

> . . . Being on the chapter of grievance which believe me dear
> Fox with you is a very hateful discussion to me I will unpack
> my mind at once . . . I take that office without the slightest
> feeling of obligation to anyone living perhaps I might say more
> – it is seventeen years since when you professed to me that I
> should not be content to accept that alone – I come directly to
> my point – and that is *my son* . . . I had a very distinct pledge
> from you that Tom should be taken care of . . . How does it
> end? You turn me over with a note to Lord Grenville . . . In
> one word, if nothing can be done for my son, the Grenville
> administration are perfectly welcome to dispose of my office.

In the end a place was found for Tom with Lord Moira in
Ireland, but that was far from ending Sheridan's concern for his
son, whose health, moreover, was all too obviously precarious.

Pitt had died in January; Fox followed him in September. It
was still Sheridan, despite those often-sharp differences over
latter years, who was put in charge of the funeral arrangements,
as he had been long ago for those of Garrick. But already, when it
became obvious that Fox was dying, Sheridan had been looking
ahead. Fox for twenty-two years had represented the constituency of Westminster, whose franchise for those days was remarkably democratic, and Sheridan longed to fight and win that seat
above all others. And he still saw himself, despite the known
mistrust of old party colleagues and despite his well-publicized
personal foibles – particularly his habitual drunkenness – as
Fox's natural successor. Now therefore he publicly put himself
forward for Westminster, only to find that Lord Grenville (Prime
Minister) and the Duke of Northumberland (one of the powerful

Whig magnificos) had agreed that Northumberland's young son, Lord Percy, should contest the vacancy. Sheridan was 'surprised and hurt'. 'Did I ever authorize you', he demanded of the Duke's business manager, 'to inform Lord Grenville that I had abandoned the idea of offering myself?'

When Parliament was dissolved in October 1806 the Duke, though remaining disgusted with both Sheridan and Grenville, withdrew his son's candidature, and Sheridan stood, supported by public subscription. After a stormy campaign he was returned, but what the Foxite faithful thought of it all emerges very clearly from the comments of Fox's nephew Lord Holland, even if we do not need to swallow all of them whole:

. . . He thought, in his inordinate vanity, that he might defy the Court, the aristocracy, and the reformers, and such was his confidence in his own personal popularity and management that he not only neglected but derided and insulted the clubs and committees through whose agency Mr Fox's election had been generally secured. He was bitterly deceived. Our party supported him very feebly. He was absolutely execrated by the people. With great exertion I obtained for him some reluctant assistance from the Ministry, and he was with much difficulty brought in as a second member to Sir Samuel Hood . . .

Worse was to come. The short-lived 'Talents' ministry fell in the spring of 1807, and consequently Sheridan not only lost his post (and salary and residence) as Navy Treasurer but, putting up again for Westminster, was beaten, and badly beaten, by the radicals Burdett and Cochrane. Conveniently, the Prince of Wales, who indirectly controlled the borough of Ilchester, found him a seat there which gave him secure Commons tenure for the next five years, but there is no doubt that he felt humiliated and embittered by his Westminster experiences. Looking back on them later, he declared:

. . . It was a real misfortune which I could never get over. It was my total ruin as a public man. It put my reputation to the test with the people, and has put me out of conceit with the labours of my life . . . Besides, I abandoned my old friends at Stafford in preferring the seat at Westminster, and the Stafford people, in throwing out my son, have left me in despair.

One of Hester's letters to the Prince of Wales shows that she too had fallen into something like despair – though it is only fair in reading it to remember that Sheridan never touched the interest, or of course the capital, belonging to her marriage settlement, and that when she died, so shortly after her husband, she was worth £40,000, which her son inherited. Still, there is no mistaking the distress behind what follows here. It is undated, but the address 'Somerset Place' is date enough, and a subsequent dated letter (February 1808) refers to the Prince's goodness in giving advice and assistance *two years ago*, presumably in response to this cry for help:

I am out of all heart and hope. – I cannot get a farthing from S. for any one thing, and I have but too much reason to think he has forestalled everything . . . Wretched and oppressed as I feel, I cannot help again looking to you for comfort and advice. I ask for no luxuries, I wish for none. I require only the necessaries for a gentlewoman and the means of having my friends about me, and the *very few* debts I have incurr'd discharged. Is it to be believed that with S.'s income I should fret myself sick for two or three hundred pounds? . . . You do not know, Sir, what a joyous nature I once had, what unbounded courage and spirits – but who can stand so many years of uncertainty, suspense and worry, and when other miseries make me so ill able to bear it? . . . The complicated state of Sheridan's affairs, I fear beyond calculation, destroys him for everything, and renders the most exalted talents in the world almost useless. From feelings of vanity, he will not let his affairs see daylight; could he be persuaded to do so, all *might* perhaps be well – at least I am told that it might – but you alone, Sir, can do it.

Sheridan's relations with the Prince, usually so good, always met difficulty when the perennial question arose of Catholic emancipation. It was obviously a matter of vital importance to Ireland, but also emphatically to Sheridan himself both as an Irishman and (in this respect at least) as a Whig. There were other less crucial matters, both private and political, which occasionally led to misunderstandings between Sheridan and his 'master' (it was *his* word). More than once over these years he felt the need to write justifying his political stance, fully admitting that he owed his parliamentary seat entirely to the Prince's goodness, insisting always on the right to speak his mind. Thus, for instance, to the Prince in July 1808: 'One day when I had the honor of accidentally meeting your Royal Highness on horseback in Oxford St though your manner was as usual gracious and kind to me, yet you said that I appear'd to have deserted you privately and POLITICALLY'. The long explanatory letter emphasizes the 'unpurchaseable consistency and sincerity' of his political principles, excuses his own 'nervous procrastinating nature', and pleads 'great and oppressive embarrassments' before ending thus:

> You have the truth and my heart before you – you cannot be on half terms with me. If I have seriously offended you, I have lost what I never will attempt to repair or recover, the favour of a Prince and future Sovereign, and you Sir will have lost what I trust and hope to God you may repair the next hour, the service and devotion of a man not a professing sycophant to your station and power, but a sincere and affectionate servant and friend to your happiness and glory.

One of the 'oppressive embarrassments', which the Prince's own enormous and chronic indebtedness should have amply qualified him to understand, was the awkward fact that the Sheridans now, in the winter and spring of 1808, had nowhere of their own to live while in London. Knowing that if he took a house, bailiffs would surely come and remove his belongings, Sheridan lived at No 7 Great George Street which belonged to Peter Moore, a good friend who had chaired the supporting committee for the Westminster election. By 1809 the Sheridan address is being given as 'Queen Street', though reference to the 'garrison' there, in a letter to the Drury Lane treasurer, surely implies precautions being taken once more against bailiffs; and for much of that year his letters bear the address 'Randalls', the farm property he rented near Polesden Lacey. Sheridan never at this period of his life lived in his major property at Polesden Lacey at all; it was let. Briefly during 1811–12 he would be occupying No 6 Cavendish Square, where his close neighbour at No 2, Lady Bessborough – her earlier tender feelings towards him when she was Lady Duncannon having been long extinguished – noted ironically, 'We shall live together I suppose.' 'Pray now don't dislike the house in C. Square,' Sheridan wrote to his 'dearest Hecca'. 'You wanted some place where you could have a little musick of an evening and upon my soul I do not pay so much for it as Tom receives for his mansion in South Audley St.' All these addresses by no means exhaust the list of his places of residence over these few years alone. We find 'Grosvenor Place' again, and – ominously – 'Cook's Hotel', before seeing that by April 1812 he has even gone back to Bruton Street.

Long before that time the list of his misfortunes had grown. On 24 February 1809 he was in the Commons as usual. In mid-debate that night the House's attention wandered from the speaking member when mutterings, and then more general cries of 'Fire!' were heard. It was learned that Drury Lane was alight. A member suggested that the House ought to adjourn, but Sheridan 'with much calmness' said he did not think that the calamity, however great, warranted such a proceeding. He was then driven to Drury Lane and saw the completeness of the destruction. It was an immense blaze: 'tremendously *grand*', said one who watched it – and another, 'It perfectly illuminated

Lincoln's Inn Fields with the brightness of day.' Everything was lost except a few things from Mrs Jordan's room, the patent document, and some of the financial records. The sacred relics went with the rest: Elizabeth Sheridan's harpsichord, sentimentally treasured by her husband; Garrick's clock, which had been ceremoniously wound up once a year, and one of the boards he had trod, saved from the earlier building. There was irony in that at the new theatre's opening fifteen years before much had been made on the first night of the excellently up-to-date fire precautions newly installed.

In the Piazza Coffee House near by, Sheridan sat and watched his livelihood disappear – for the theatre had been insured for only £35,000, perhaps a tenth of its estimated 1809 value. Someone in the coffee house remarked on his composure. 'A man', observed Sheridan, 'may surely take a glass of wine by his own fireside.' And the next day, 'stealing from a croud' to write to his 'heart's beloved Hecca', he claimed, though it can hardly have been true, that he was 'not greatly moved':

> Had I felt this blow as many would have done, so may God judge my heart if every trace of regret would not have been driven from my mind by the real pain which your account of yourself has given me. Only *you* be well and I will surmount everything but without you – there is nothing I wish to struggle for . . . Tomorrow morning . . . at Epsom . . . there shall be horses ready to bring you to Queen Street, and to your affectionate and unalter'd friend and husband R.B.S.

Within a short time the Drury Lane company managed temporarily to take over the Lyceum Theatre, and there again in the following season Tom Sheridan, after a stay in Madeira for his health, returned as one of the joint managers. But already within three months of the fire there was talk of a committee being formed to produce plans for rebuilding Drury Lane and, at Sheridan's request, Samuel Whitbread became a member of it – soon the leading member. Whitbread was a friend of his, Grey's brother-in-law, and a family connection of Hester's. He had been on the committee organizing subscriptions to support Sheridan's candidature at Westminster, and he had long been a trustee of the Polesden estate and of the Sheridan marriage settlement. A wealthy brewer, he was prominent in Parliament as one of the more radically inclined Whigs.

Sheridan now wrote to him with that indestructible optimism of his: 'I have work'd the whole subject in my mind; and see a clear way to retrieve a great property, at least for my son and his family.' He had become ill soon after the fire and, not being seen in the Commons for a considerable time – a very rare thing for him – he was even reported in some papers to be dead. Eulogies were printed, 'written' so the *Monthly Mirror* suggested (but without evidence) 'by himself'. He 'went down the next day', the article continued, 'to assure them that *he was not dead*, but nobody would believe him.' But this illness was obviously much on his mind as he now approached Whitbread: 'Assist me', he begged, 'in relieving my mind from the greatest affliction such a situation can produce – the fears of others suffering by my death.'

Whitbread's acceptance of responsibility for co-ordinating the complicated double-plan of paying off as far as practicable the enormous debts of the old Drury Lane and raising the money for building a new one, meant that in Sheridan's latter years he was to become a figure of looming importance. His passage from the position of friend and rescuer to that of worst enemy, reproached and blamed for each new misfortune, makes painful reading, capped as it is at last (and at least part of the cause was worry over the legal threats arising from new Drury Lane debts incurred under his management) by the tragic story of Whitbread's suicide in 1815.

Sheridan's financial predicament had always resembled that of the tight-rope performer crossing Niagara in a stiff breeze. After the fire his feet had lost contact; he was hanging on by his fingers. The only substantial money left to him now being the Duchy of Cornwall sinecure, it is not surprising to find him soon in marital crisis once again. Twice before this, Mrs Sheridan had been reduced to begging the theatre treasurer to send her money to pay her washerwoman; and now, a gentlewoman accustomed to expensive living and faced with she knew not what fresh deprivations, she wrote to her husband listing her fears and grievances, making suggestions for managing in future, and offering to separate *if that would bring him happiness*. Sheridan's reply is more than a reply; it is a most revealing document, well over 4,000 words long; an apologia. For once she is 'Dear Hester', not 'Heart's beloved Hecca'; but he refuses to quarrel and will not lodge counter-claims.

He asks 'pardon for every embarrassment and distress' she has suffered, while requesting her to concede that they can hardly be compared with his own: recently, he confesses, he has had to stoop 'for the first time to solicit and accept the pecuniary assistance of private friendship'. He admits to being negligent, forgetful, procrastinating, over-sanguine – but not neglectful, *never* neglectful. He reviews the extremely generous terms of her marriage settlement; the inviolability of her jointure (not to be touched till it accumulated to at least £40,000); various heavy drains recently on his purse; how from 'honourable pride' when so briefly Navy Treasurer he paid £2,000 from his salary, and £3,600 more besides, voluntarily to satisfy claims from Drury Lane debenture-holders; and the very considerable monies expended – and more to be expected of him in future – to help sustain Tom and pay off *his* debts. He shows how Polesden (which she must not forget will be inherited by his other son, *her* son, Charles) has lost him '7 or £8000'. But then, wildly optimistic as ever amid the encircling gloom, he sketches the solvent, almost the rosy, future. His friend Peter Moore has agreed to advance enough to settle her debts and will guarantee future payment of Charles's school fees at Winchester. Under changed arrangements the new theatre ought to bring in thirty guineas a week (five guineas per performance) as the old used to. Then there will be his share of compensation for losses by the fire. Further, his Duchy income should produce – he does not explain how – '3 or £400 a year over and above what it has brought in previously'. All in all, he ought to be receiving £4,000 a year. As for talk of separation:

> I plainly answer that such an act would be follow'd on my part by my instantly taking my boy with me to some corner of the earth and be no more heard of till my death should be by him announced to you, after I should think no very protracted period . . .

He was not going to deny himself the right to enjoy *some* self-esteem, or to remember acts of 'kindness, gentleness, and benevolence', and so he ends:

> You will forgive my having said thus much of myself . . . It may be egotism but it is a fact . . . And now God bless you and as I trust you will have pardoned whatever you have thought amiss in my conduct so do I from my soul forgive you.

Towards the end of that year George III's mind, tormented by the mortal illness of his favourite daughter Amelia, once more became deranged, so that again the regency problem stood at the forefront of domestic politics and the old question arose: what powers ought the Prince to wield as Regent, and what restrictions, if any, should be imposed? The Tory government of Perceval in December 1810 introduced a bill proposing limitations which followed Pitt's proposals in the 1788–9 regency crisis, though the new bill was to apply for twelve months only, to allow for the chance of the King's recovering.

Once more the Whigs were in a turmoil – mostly of pleasurable anticipation, for the Prince had been reckoned their friend ever since he began hobnobbing with Fox and the young men of Brooks's nearly thirty years before. As the youthful Palmerston now hopefully remarked, 'We are all on the kick and go.' The Whig leaders at this point (with Fox's nephew Lord Holland in close attendance) were Charles (now Earl) Grey and William,

Lord Grenville, brother both of the Marquis of Buckingham and of Sheridan's friend from early days, Tom Grenville. Grey had long mistrusted, and of late positively disliked, even despised, Sheridan. Grenville, who had changed horses since 1788–9 when he supported strict limitations, was unloved generally – indeed a member of one of the country's *most* unloved, if politically most powerful, families, always hungry for honours and status, great chasers after office and rich sinecures. If Grey despised Sheridan, Sheridan certainly despised Grenville, and by this time had lost most of his earlier regard for Grey. When, therefore, the Prince was called on to make a formal response to the message concerning the regency sent him by Parliament, it was Grey and Grenville, as governmental heirs apparent, who expected to draft and indeed did make the first draft of the Prince's answer. But still there was Sheridan in the wings – Sheridan, whose Elizabeth in her own neat hand had made the fair copy of her husband's reply, compiled on behalf of the Prince, to the parallel parliamentary message of twenty-two years before. Sheridan, Lord Moira, and the Prince's legal adviser, Adam, behaved now as a kind of Carlton House kitchen cabinet. They mulled over the Grey-Grenville document, and Sheridan who did not like it (neither did the Prince) made important revisions in it. Then he and Adam took their version to Holland House – Sheridan, according to Lord Holland, 'flushed with wine' – and had an acrimonious session concerning it with Grey and Grenville.

Both sides in this dispute later wrote defences of their conduct, Sheridan's marked 'Read and approved by the Prince, January 20, 1811', while the Whig lords complained with barely concealed anger that their 'humble endeavours' had been 'submitted to the judgement of another person' whose advice had been taken although *they*, 'however unworthily', had been 'honoured with your Royal Highness's commands'.

Even before this incident Sheridan and the Whig establishment stood far apart. After it the break was complete. He was never forgiven, and even though the Whigs could hardly pin all the blame on him for their ultimate discomfiture in the new ministry-making, they deeply resented the fact that while the Regent fell increasingly out of sympathy with them (and in the end kept a Tory administration), it was noted that Sheridan was still for some time welcome at Carlton House. They suspected that he at least regarded himself still as one of the Prince's special advisers. When in May 1812 the Prime Minister, Perceval, was assassinated, Sheridan, seen visiting Carlton House, was rumoured to be meddling again, this time in the business of forming a new ministry. In fact, as one of his letters to the Regent demonstrates, he was advising *against* the exclusion of Grey from a projected ministry (which did not materialize) to be led by Lord Wellesley. In the event it was Lord Liverpool who came in as Prime Minister, and was to stay so for the next fifteen years. The Regent's ostensible explanation for standing by the Tories, after all, was his preference for adhering to their vigorous Peninsular War policy and their resistance to Catholic emancipation. In fact he had become less and less inclined to the Whigs ever since the death of Fox, and the exclusion of Sheridan from their counsels ended the chapter of the Prince's personal links with them. By 1812 he had become as Tory-minded as any country squire or the new ministry itself.

Sheridan now determined on what proved a fatal gamble. Although he repeatedly professed certainty that in the forthcoming election the Prince would be glad to bring him in again for Ilchester (and Tom too, as the second member), he resolved not to stand there. Instead he would put up as a fully independent candidate for Stafford, the constituency which until 1806 he had represented for twenty-six years. The prospect excited him: *'My heart is in the thing and if I start I will not be beat, by God.'* As for the money needed for the fight, 'thousands upon thousands' were due to him from the Drury Lane settlement, whose terms indeed had now been agreed. Sheridan was assessed to receive £28,000 gross (and Tom Sheridan £12,000) – after that quarter of the theatre's total debts which it was going to be practicable to settle had been paid off. But from that £28,000, as Whitbread had to remind him, must be subtracted the value of many claims outstanding against him, including those from the Linley family and Peter Moore. And Whitbread further stipulated that Sheridan should take a large part of his payment in bonds, 'in trust to answer events' – whereas of course what Sheridan needed, as ever, and needed badly, was ready cash.

The bitterest aspect of the settlement, however, was the committee's decision that the Sheridans were to be allowed no part in running the *new* Drury Lane. As Whitbread put it brutally to Tom, the very name of Sheridan, if associated with the project, would be enough to frighten investment away. Sheridan, asked to 'stand aloof', took the rebuff personally, and took it hard. But still there were those 'thousands upon thousands' due to him, and all he wanted immediately from Whitbread was an advance of £2,000 in order to contest Stafford. Whitbread, a prudent guardian of other people's money, refused it. He 'deeply lamented' Sheridan's distress and was ready to contribute privately his 'mite' to alleviate it, but the 'palliation' proposed was not in his power to offer. A public fund must not be used for largesse.

Sheridan's constitution was sturdy and his health had been generally reliable, but frequently now there comes talk of illness, some of it a little mysterious. 'I continue very unwell,' he writes, 'and the progressive state of my varicose veins, my secret alarming complaint, preys on my hopes and spirits, for I never will have to do with any operation.' He tells Lady Holland he has had a violent cough and for 'two nights a pain in my side which I hate above all things'. And again, 'I was too ill even to be able to remain in the House.' Anticipating no doubt a reproof from Hester for his drinking too much, he writes to her, 'I am very unwell myself and have lost all power of sleeping and yet upon my soul I drink little wine.' And to Tom, 'God bless you I am as tired as a dog.'

Ever-multiplying infirmities and other distresses, both his and his wife's, would henceforth draw them, of necessity, closer together. There is no more talk of separation, and indeed towards the end of 1811 Hester was writing to Lord Holland '. . . I never can see him as *deeply wounded* as I have seen him lately . . . The disagreement between him and Whitbread hurts me more than I can express.' There came a further and severe wound at the October 1812 election in Stafford. Although without his £2,000 from Whitbread's committee, he stood and he lost.

So the House of Commons, without knowing it, had heard Sheridan speak for the last time. Fittingly, almost his final words there had been on Ireland and its Catholics:

> My objection to the present ministry is that they are avowedly arrayed and embodied against a principle – that of concession to the Catholics of Ireland – which I think, and must always think, essential to the safety of the empire . . . In fine, I think the situation of Ireland a paramount consideration. If they were to be the last words I should ever utter in this House, I should say, 'Be just to Ireland, as you value your honour. Be just to Ireland, as you value your own peace.'

12

Desperate last days

THE rebuilt Drury Lane opened in that same October of
1812 with an address of some seventy lines by Byron,
spoken from the stage, recalling how the fire of three years back
shook 'its red shadow o'er the startled Thames', celebrating the
great names both of decades past 'ere Garrick fled or Brinsley
ceased to write', and also of more recent days – Mrs Siddons,
whose thrilling art 'o'erwhelmed the gentlest, stormed the
sternest heart'; 'Roscius' too, who 'sighed his last thanks, and
wept his last adieu':

> The curtain rises, may our stage unfold
> Scenes not unworthy Drury's days of old!

Sheridan refused to attend, and even when a melodrama, *The
Russian*, by Tom Sheridan, was staged there the following May,
he declined to be present. Staying at a hotel near the theatre, he
wrote to the manager, 'Send me word how the play has gone off
truly and sincerely . . . I am most anxious for its success . . . you
know I do not enter your d—d theatre.' Tom's play achieved a
tolerable eleven performances, but Tom himself was increasingly
in a bad way, with difficulty in breathing after only the slightest
exertion, and 'miserably thin and weak'. The next year he would
be off with his wife and one daughter to the Cape of Good Hope.

It was heartbreaking for Sheridan to be in his company: 'I spend all the time with him I can,' he told Hester, 'as he seems to wish it, but he so reminds me of his mother, and his feeble, gasping way of speaking deprives me of all hope.'

There was a bleak outlook in whichever direction he turned. A letter to Tom in July 1815, the month after Waterloo:

> . . . Politics I am sick of. The Prince I know nothing of. Party is a cheat, Stafford worse, and the theatre and the conduct towards me I hate to think of. In addition there is one subject which has heavily weigh'd on my mind for these last six months – watching by a sick couch with the most gloomy apprehensions . . . was hard work to my nerves even in my stout days. – The plain truth is, whatever you may have heard from others, that Hester has been for the last six months and *is* in a very dangerous way.

In fact she was already suffering from the cancer which would kill her in four years' time.

'Sick of politics' he might be; reliance on a Prince Regent with Tory ministers he did not expect; yet in May 1814 he decided to stand once more for Westminster, as an independent but with the influential backing of the Duke of Norfolk. The Duke was that same 'Jockey' Norfolk who twenty-five years before had lent him his country mansion at Deepdene in Surrey which had served as a place to which Elizabeth in particular might escape from the turmoil of fashionable London. Again now, friends and sympathizers were coming to Sheridan's aid with offers to lend him their houses. Richard Ironmonger, the owner of Randall Farm, Leatherhead, where Sheridan had spent many months during 1808 and 1809, let him have the place again for a long stay, and Lord Wellesley gave him the use of 17 Savile Row, which was to prove the final item in the long catalogue of Sheridan's London addresses.

The parliamentary vacancy had arisen because Cochrane, one of the Westminster members, had been expelled from the

Commons – as it turned out unwarrantably – for fraud. Sheridan's opponents promised to be Major Cartwright, a leading campaigner for parliamentary reform, and Henry Brougham, a future Lord Chancellor; but this time there were to be no excitements at the hustings, for Cochrane's name was cleared and he was re-elected. Sheridan withdrew. Had he stood against Brougham, he would have enjoyed the Prince's continued, even enthusiastic, support, since at this time Brougham was championing the cause of the Prince's most hated enemy, his wife.*

If Sheridan had won re-election to the Commons, one at least of his nightmares would have disappeared. As a Member of Parliament he could not have been arrested for debt, but out of Parliament he was unprotected. On four occasions between 1813 and 1815 he is reported by various not always reliable sources to have been arrested and locked up in a sponging house (a bailiff's lodging-house for debtors before their committal to prison). At least once he quite certainly was – in May 1814, when from Tooke's Court, Cursitor Street, off Chancery Lane, he addressed a bitterly accusing letter to Whitbread, at whose Bedfordshire home he had only recently been a guest for a month-long stay. Now he protested:

> You have no right to keep me here. For it is in truth *your* act . . . There are still thousands and thousands due to me both legally and equitably from the theatre – my word ought to be taken on this subject . . . O God! with what mad confidence I have trusted your word – I ask justice from you and no boon . . .

Whitbread had recently become more reluctant than ever to

---

* Caroline of Brunswick, the Protestant princess he had rashly elected to marry in 1795, she being the price he was at that time prepared to pay to secure a doubling of his annual allowance and a settlement of his £630,000 debts. His association with the Catholic Mrs Fitzherbert had some time previously been quietly dropped.

'Breakfast party given by Mr Samuel Rogers', by Charles Mottram.
Included in this assembly of eminent literary and artistic figures of 1815
are: standing at the extreme left, John Flaxman and Sir Walter Scott;
standing fifth from left, Sydney Smith; standing centre background,
Washington Irving. Seated, from the left: Sheridan, Thomas Moore,

William Wordsworth, Robert Southey, Samuel Taylor Coleridge (seated centre background). Seated centre foreground: Samuel Rogers; to his right, Byron and John Kemble. The group standing on the right of the picture includes Thomas Lawrence (third from right) and J.M.W. Turner (second from right).

agree a final settlement with Sheridan because he was alarmed by threats emanating from William Taylor, manager of the King's Theatre, Haymarket. Taylor, years before, had lodged a demand against Sheridan for £20,000 – a claim which as early as 1811 Sheridan had volunteered to submit to arbitration.

From the sponging-house he was soon released, but whether by Whitbread's own intervention or another's (possibly even the Prince Regent's) is not clear. If it was Whitbread, it was against the advice of Mrs Sheridan, who wrote to him:

> Sheridan's state of mind kills me – all I can say to him seems to poison his mind. Clarke [her doctor] has given me leave to go and see him . . . tell me then where I am to direct the coachman – Do not refuse this . . . and above all things do not go to him yourself . . .

Six months later Sheridan, still waiting for his money, attacked again: 'You thought fit to tie up £12,000 of my property, by which I lost my seat in Parliament, God forgive you!' He was writing then from North Court, Shorwell, in the Isle of Wight, where his brothers-in-law had arranged a long stay for Hester to give her health a better chance. Sheridan himself spent a good deal of time with her there during 1814 and 1815. The Hampshire coast opposite the Island was Ogle territory, and on various occasions he enjoyed sailing excursions with different members of the fraternity and their families. (There were four Ogle brothers.) For pleasure it was difficult to beat skimming over the Solent or Southampton Water on a fine summer's day in a 'yatch', and it was from Cowes – where however one might find the Marine Hotel 'damned noisy' – that in July 1814 he reported cheerfully that he and Hester had just landed 'after a pleasant sail, which has done her infinite good'. The cheerfulness, alas, proved only temporary.

To raise ready cash he was now reduced occasionally to begging a loan from a friend, which pride had earlier forbidden; there were at different times requests to Fitzpatrick, Canning,

Peter Moore, Tom Grenville, Sir John Hippisley, Samuel Rogers, and perhaps others. The Duke of Bedford generously relinquished old claims for Drury Lane rent, and lent £200 besides. Sheridan raised money too, in a grudging fury, by selling some of his pictures; six of them, including two Morlands and two Gainsboroughs, went for £660. The celebrated Reynolds portrait of his first wife as St Cecilia by now belonged to his solicitor, Burgess, but at about this time Sheridan engaged Beechey to make a copy for him. He 'grieved' for the sacrifice of his pictures; however, he kept telling himself and telling his friends, Burgess among them, and telling even his wife sometimes, but with sadly less conviction, 'We shall come through.'

He divided his time now mainly between the Isle of Wight, Leatherhead, and Savile Row; Leatherhead because it was near to Polesden, and hence convenient as a headquarters from which to oversee the affairs of his estate, with its tenant farms. Hester's nephew relates how, when he stayed with him at Leatherhead at this time, Sheridan 'rose early, and after breakfast proceeded in his barouche to his estate, over a portion of which he walked each day, making minute inquiries relating to his affairs, over which he seemed very anxious'. From Leatherhead in the spring of 1815, still a Surrey proprietor, a rural landlord however impoverished, sitting at a table on which were 'three samples of lamb's wool' and 'a hatful of Polesden violets', he writes to Whitbread again: 'God forgive you all in your curs'd City.' But he finds time to advise him on a matter where theatre business and farming interests might mingle. There had recently been rioting by the poor against the proposed new corn law so urgently demanded by the farmers and landowners, and Whitbread's Drury Lane was about to stage *Richard III*. 'Beware, and listen to the wise,' wrote Sheridan. 'Keep politics out of the theatre.' He feared that certain 'allusions' in the play, unless they were edited out, might be taken topically and prove inflammatory. 'Any mischief will be laid at your door.' Yet, he admitted, what a fine part for Edmund Kean, Drury Lane's latest young star – his Shylock had just made a sensation there. Sheridan's particular admiration for Kean stemmed from an occasion, the year before, when he had invited him home to Savile Row to read *Othello* to an ill Mrs Sheridan. As he then pronounced, 'He exceeds all I have heard.' Iago and Othello were among Kean's greatest parts. Listening to him, said Coleridge, was 'like reading Shakespeare by flashes of lightning'.

Early in 1815, probably for the first time since its opening, Sheridan must have gone back to Drury Lane, for he writes to his wife, 'The actors wanted to give me a fine dinner, but I declined it – it would have been great dudgeon to Whitbread.' However, by July Whitbread had committed suicide, and there was soon a new management, among whose first productions was *The Duenna*. One night when Kean was playing, Sheridan allowed himself to be persuaded to attend. The friend who accompanied him, Lord Essex, missing him in the interval, eventually discovered him in the green-room, where, with 'a sort of filial cordiality' the players drank to his health. On parting with Essex that night in Savile Row Sheridan 'said triumphantly that the world would soon hear of him, for the Duke of Norfolk was about to bring him into Parliament'. The basis for this expectation is at once confirmed and shown to be destroyed by his words a few days later, when he had just been told that the Duke was critically ill, and likely to die – and indeed he did die soon afterwards: 'He had just settled a plan to give me a seat without expence,' Sheridan told Hester – adding that Norfolk knew 'my condition of being my absolute master . . . but poor Dan he meets with many disappointments lately'.

Just before Sheridan died in July 1816, his friend the Irish singer Michael Kelly, hearing that he was in abject straits and lacking basic necessities, sent for Sheridan's one remaining manservant to learn from him the true state of affairs. He was told that nothing was wanting, and therefore concluded that reports had been falsely circulated 'for the purpose of scandal' in order to blacken the names of Sheridan's rich friends and old associates who should have come to the rescue but had not. Moreover, after his father had died Charles Sheridan informed his stepbrother (then holding the office of Treasurer at the newly conquered

Cape Colony) that their father's death was unaccompanied by suffering and that reports of privations were unfounded. Some accounts of these privations are, however, persuasively circumstantial. There was some squalor; bare reception rooms; filth and stench everywhere; Sheridan in a truckle-bed in a garret with something resembling a horse-cloth over him; just a trunk beside the bed for Lady Bessborough to sit on when she came to visit him, only to be terrified by the dying man's gruesome conversation. (She sent him £20.)

Charles Sheridan's comforting message to Tom at the Cape must have been to some extent misleading – just how much so it is not easy to be sure about in view of evidence often coloured either by party prejudice or wounded family pride. But, necessary allowances being made, there remains a residue of well-attested fact.

Six months before his death Sheridan was suffering from multiple disorders: 'ist my poor veins – my first terror – 2nd the inflammation . . . 3rd my total lack of appetite . . . and 4th this racking cough . . . If I cannot walk I can have no exercise, if no exercise no sleep . . . and how can this last? . . .' Thomas Moore tells of the 'diseased state of the stomach' and also, darkly, of 'an abscess . . . distressingly situated'. 'Never again', Sheridan begged his wife, 'let one harsh word pass between us during this period, which may not be long, that we are in this world together.' Shortly after that was written, Hester finally returned to Savile Row. As late as May 1816 Sheridan, though very ill, was not wholly confined to bed, for on the ninth of that month he was writing to his 'good friend' John Graham, sheriff's broker and auctioneer: 'Fail me not tomorrow – dinner at three.' But by then it is clear that he was more deeply than ever, and this time desperately, in the toils of bailiffs and brokers' men, for, on the very 'tomorrow' of his note and the following day, Graham's auctioneer partner George Hindle – 'that dirty thief Hindle' – had engaged, and advertised, to sell Sheridan's furniture and effects just up the road in Savile Place.

Among those who kept in touch was the poet, wit, and literary panjandrum Samuel Rogers, who was a friend also of Byron and a prominent member of the Holland House circle. When Rogers brought Lord Holland to visit Sheridan at Savile Row, both men volunteered to help in whatever practical way they could – and although the Regent's friend J.W. Croker later implied slightingly that the Hollands' assistance was limited to 'ice and currant water' this was probably unfair. A few days later Rogers happened to have with him Thomas Moore, the Irish poet and man of letters who was to write the first life of Sheridan. It was just after midnight when a message arrived from Sheridan, in his own unique blend of optimism and panic:

> I find things settled so that £150 will remove all difficulties. I am absolutely undone and broken-hearted. I shall negotiate for publication of the plays successfully in the course of a week, when all shall be returned . . .
>
> They are going to put the carpets out of the window, and break into Mrs S's room and *take me* – for God's sake let me see you.

Moore and Rogers hurried immediately to Savile Row. Being then assured by the servant that all was safe for the night, Moore went along next morning with Rogers's draft for £150, but of course this was far from removing 'all difficulties'. Sheridan's condition meanwhile worsened until he was completely bedridden. An article in the *Morning Post* publicized his wretched state, and called for immediate help rather than praise, honour, and a fine funeral later. Towards the end of June George Canning sent him £100, with the offer a few days later of a junior clerkship for Charles at the Board of Control. The Prince Regent, informed in some detail of his forlorn predicament by one John Taylor Vaughan, sent him as an emissary to Sheridan with £200 – and there is reason to suppose that more would have been available, but even the £200 was not accepted. In Moore's words:

> . . . The proposition being submitted to Mrs Sheridan, that

lady, after consulting with some of her relatives, returned for answer that, as there was a sufficiency of means to provide all that was necessary for her husband's comfort, as well as her own, she begged leave to decline the offer.

Moore also testified that, contrary to some accounts, Mrs Sheridan, 'though drooping herself with an illness that did not leave her long behind him, watched over his every word and wish, with unremitting anxiety to the last.' Just what 'sufficiency of means' was forthcoming from the Ogles must remain obscure. What is beyond question is that that good old friend of Sheridan's, Dr Bain, once intervened towards the end to prevent his desperately ill patient being carried from the house by force. A sheriff's officer was about to make the arrest and remove Sheridan in his blankets, when he was told that, if he did, Bain would personally see that he was prosecuted for murder. When Sheridan died on 7 July, the bailiffs were still in possession in the hall downstairs, smoking and passing their time by playing cards.

Ten years before his death, just after he had been at the simple funeral of his first wife's youngest sister Jane, he had expressed a wish that his own might be similarly quiet. He contrasted then the dignity of the ceremony for Jane with 'the gaudy parade and show' there had been at Elizabeth's, all the way from Bristol to Wells Cathedral, and afterwards 'the mob, high and low', crowding round the vault. The recollection of it, he said, had always given him pain.

His own funeral, with its procession from Peter Moore's house in Great George Street to Poets' Corner in Westminster Abbey, the Duke of Bedford and five other peers acting as pall-bearers, paid fitting respect to one of the age's leading men without being at all a 'gaudy parade'. Still, Thomas Moore and others were critical. Moore had been told that Poets' Corner was Sheridan's 'aversion' – he would have liked to have been placed near Fox; and about the ceremony itself Moore remained bitter. Of the very impressive array of rank who followed the coffin, 'Where were they all while any life remained in him?' he demanded – not quite fairly in view of many of the facts now known. 'Why all this parade of regret and homage over his tomb?'

One at least who did have a right to regret and homage was Byron, who two or three years earlier had seen a good deal of Sheridan round Samuel Rogers's breakfast table and on other convivial occasions. He had warmed to him, grown to love and respect him. 'Poor dear Sherry!' he wrote. 'I shall never forget the day he and Rogers and Moore and I passed together; when *he* talked and we listened, without one yarn, from six till one in the morning.' It was Byron who now wrote a monody on the death of Sheridan, to stand side by side with Sheridan's own on the death of Garrick, both at their due time spoken from the stage of Drury Lane Theatre.

> The flash of wit – the bright intelligence,
> The beam of song, the blaze of eloquence . . .
> Ye Bards! to whom the drama's muse is dear,
> He was your master – emulate him *here*!
> Ye men of wit and social eloquence,
> He was your brother – bear his ashes hence.

At many places in his letters and journals Byron wrote of days and nights in the company of Sheridan, drunk and sober.

> I heard Sheridan [as a public speaker] only once, and that briefly; but I liked his voice, his manner and his wit; he is the only one of them that I ever wished to hear at greater length. In society I have met him frequently; he was superb! He had a sort of liking for me, and never attacked me – at least to my face, and he did everybody else . . . Poor fellow! he got drunk very thoroughly and very soon. It occasionally fell to my lot to convoy him home – no sinecure, for he was so tipsy that I was obliged to put on his cock'd hat for him: to be sure it tumbled off again, but I was not myself so sober as to be able to pick it up again.

[204]

Byron recalled too the delicious irony of an occasion when Sheridan, taken from the gutter, all but insensible, by the watch and being asked his name replied stoutly, amid hiccups, '*Wilberforce*!' – that most earnest of campaigners against vice and irreligion.

One does not look to find Horace Walpole in the company of Byron, but in their estimation of Sheridan they stand side by side. 'Mr Sheridan', wrote Walpole in his old age to his young friend John Pinkerton,

> is one of the most perfect comic writers I know, and unites the most uncommon of qualities – his plots are sufficiently deep, without the clumsy intanglement, the muddy profundity of Congreve – characters strictly in nature – wit without affectation . . . What talents! The complete orator in the senate, or in Westminster Hall – and the excellent dramatist in the most difficult province of the drama.

Whatever Sheridan had done, said Byron, had been 'par excellence the best of its kind': the best comedy (*The School for Scandal*), the best opera (*The Duenna* – far better, Byron thought, than the *The Beggar's Opera*), the best farce (*The Critic* – 'only it is too good for a farce'), the best address (the *Monody on Garrick*) and to crown all, the very best oration (the Begum Speech) ever heard in this country. Sheridan wept when somebody passed on to him these opinions of Byron's – which, when Byron heard about it, caused him to say that he was more pleased to have said what he said than to have written the *Iliad*: 'Poor fellow, his very dregs are better than the first sprightly runnings of others.'

When Moore first began planning his biography, it was Byron who wrote to him with some advice:

> The life of such a man may be made far more amusing than if he had been a Wilberforce – and this without offending the living or insulting the dead. The Whigs abuse him; however,

[205]

he never left them, and such blunderers deserve neither credit nor compassion. As for his creditors – remember, Sheridan *never had* a shilling, and was thrown, with great powers and passions, into the thick of the world, and placed upon the pinnacle of success, with no other external means to support him in his elevation. Did Fox . . . pay *his* debts? Was the [Prince of Wales's] drunkenness more excusable than his? Were his intrigues more notorious than those of all his contemporaries? and is his memory to be blasted and theirs respected? Don't let yourself be led away by clamour . . . for he beat them all *out* and *out*. Never mind the lies of the humbug Whigs. Recollect that he was an Irishman and a clever fellow, and that *we* have had some very pleasant days with him. Don't forget that he was at school at Harrow, where, in my time, we used to show his name – R.B. Sheridan, 1765 – as an honour to the walls.

Bibliography

The Dramatic Works of Richard Brinsley Sheridan, ed. Cecil Price, 2 vols, Oxford University Press, 1973

The Plays and Poems of Richard Brinsley Sheridan, ed. R. Crompton Rhodes, 2 vols, Blackwell, 1928

Speeches of Richard Brinsley Sheridan, ed. 'A Constitutional Friend', 5 vols, 1816

The Letters of Richard Brinsley Sheridan, ed. Cecil Price, 3 vols, Oxford University Press, 1966

Sheridan's collected correspondence, admirably edited and annotated by Cecil Price some twenty years ago, demonstrated the truth of what had been suspected since R. Crompton Rhodes published *Harlequin Sheridan* (Blackwell, 1933) – that a good deal of what was in the earlier biographies was questionable. Two other collections of letters, *The Correspondence of George Prince of Wales* (ed. A. Aspinall, 8 vols, Cassell, 1963–71) and the letters of Lord Edward Fitzgerald (in vol. 2 of *The Correspondence of Emily Duchess of Leinster*, ed. B. Fitzgerald, Irish Manuscripts Commission, 1947–57) have further illuminated areas of previous doubt and controversy.

Three full-scale lives of Sheridan held the field for many years: those by Thomas Moore (*Memoirs of the Life of the Right Honourable Richard Brinsley Sheridan*, 2 vols, Longman, 2nd ed, 1825); by W. Fraser Rae (*Sheridan, a Biography*, 2 vols, Bentley, 1896); and by Walter Sichel (*Sheridan*, 2 vols, Constable, 1909). Moore is still valuable, not least because he knew the elderly Sheridan personally. Rae, writing at the instance of a great-grandson of Sheridan, omitted much and is monotonously laudatory. Sichel published important new material, but his 1,100-odd pages are floridly 'literary' and self-indulgently digressive.

ANGELO, H., *Reminiscences*, 2 vols, Colburn, 1828–30

AYLING, S., *George the Third*, Collins, 1972

BESSBOROUGH, EARL OF, *Extracts from the Correspondence of Georgiana Duchess of Devonshire*, John Murray, 1955

BESSBOROUGH, EARL OF, and ASPINALL, A., *Lady Bessborough and her Family Circle*, John Murray, 1940

BINGHAM, M., *Sheridan, the Track of a Comet*, Allen and Unwin, 1972

BOADEN, J., *Memoirs of the Life of John Philip Kemble*, 2 vols, Longman, 1825

BOR, M. and CLELLAND, J., *Still the Lark*, a biography of Elizabeth Linley, Merlin Press, 1962

BURKE, EDMUND, *Correspondence*, gen. ed. T.W. Copeland, 10 vols, Cambridge and Chicago University Presses, 1958–78

BUTLER, E.M., *Sheridan, a Ghost Story*, Constable, 1931

BYRON, LORD, *Letters and Diaries*, ed. P. Quennell, 2 vols, John Murray, 1950

—*Address Spoken at the Opening of Drury Lane Theatre*, and *Monody on the Death of Richard Brinsley Sheridan*, in collected poems, various editions

CREEVEY, THOMAS, *The Creevey Papers*, ed. H. Maxwell, 2 vols, John Murray, 1903

D'ARBLAY, F., *Diary and Letters*, ed. C. Barrett, 4 vols, Bickers and Son, 1876

DERRY, J. W., *Charles James Fox*, Batsford, 1972

FOTHERGILL, B., *Mrs Jordan*, Faber and Faber, 1965

FOX, C.J., *Memorials and Correspondence*, ed. Lord John Russell, 4 vols, 1853

GARRICK, DAVID, *The Letters of David Garrick*, eds D.M. Little and G.M. Kahrl, 3 vols, Oxford University Press, 1963

GIBBS, L., *Sheridan*, Dent, 1947

HAZLITT, WILLIAM, *Letters on the English Comic Writers*, Everyman edn, Dent, 1910

HOBHOUSE, C., *Fox*, John Murray, 1934

HOLLAND, LORD, *Memoirs of the Whig Party during my Time*, 2 vols, Longman, 1852–4

—*Further Memoirs of the Whig Party, 1807–21*, ed. Lord Stavordale, John Murray, 1905

KELLY, MICHAEL, *Reminiscences*, 2 vols, 1826, republished, ed. R. Fiske, Oxford University Press, 1975

LEFANU, A., *Memoirs . . . of Mrs Frances Sheridan*, Longman, 1824

LOFTIS, J., *Sheridan and the Drama of Georgian England*, Blackwell, 1977

MANVELL, R., *Sarah Siddons*, Heinemann, 1970

MARSHALL, P.J., *The Impeachment of Warren Hastings*, Oxford University Press, 1965

MAXWELL, C., *Dublin under the Georges*, Harrap and Hodges Figgis, Dublin, 1946

MINTO, SIR G. ELLIOT, EARL OF, *Life and Letters*, 3 vols, Longman, 1874

MOON, P., *Warren Hastings and British India*, Hodder and Stoughton, 1947

MOORE, THOMAS, *Memoirs, Journal and Correspondence*, ed. Lord John Russell, vol. 2 of 8 vols, Longman, 1853–6

NAMIER, SIR L., BROOKE, J., and others: *The Commons 1754–90*, 3 vols, HMSO, 1964

NICOLL, A., *A History of English Drama*, vol. 3, Cambridge University Press, 1927

ROGERS, SAMUEL, *Table Talk*, ed. A. Dyce, Johnson, 1856

SADLER, M.T.H., *The Political Career of R.B. Sheridan*, Blackwell, 1912

SHERIDAN, BETSY, *Journal*, ed. W. LeFanu, Eyre and Spottiswoode, 1960

STUART, D.M., *Dearest Bess*, Methuen, 1955

WALPOLE, HORACE, *Letters*, ed. P. Toynbee, 19 vols, Oxford University Press, 1918–25;

—*Last Journals*, ed J. Doran, 2 vols, Bodley Head, 1859

WATERHOUSE, E., *Gainsborough*, Hulton, 1958

WATSON, J.S., *The Reign of George III*, Oxford University Press, 1960

WRAXALL, N., *Historical and Posthumous Memoirs*, ed. H.B. Wheatley, 5 vols, Bickers and Son, 1884

Index

Numbers in *italics* refer to illustration captions